# beautiful
# beaded
# bags

Dorothy Wood

David & Charles

To Sorrel, who never has too many bags

A DAVID & CHARLES BOOK
David & Charles is a subsidiary of F&W (UK) Ltd.,
an F&W Publications Inc. company

First published in the UK in 2004

Reprinted 2004 (twice)

Text and designs Copyright © Dorothy Wood 2004

Distributed in North America
by F&W Publications, Inc.
4700 East Galbraith Road
Cincinnati, OH 45236
1-800-289-0963

A catalogue record for this book is available from the British Library.

ISBN 0 7153 1791 1 hardback
ISBN 0 7153 1792 X paperback

Printed in China by Hong Kong Graphics & Printing Ltd.
for David & Charles
Brunel House    Newton Abbot    Devon

Executive Editor  Cheryl Brown
Editor  Jennifer Proverbs
Art Editor  Prudence Rogers
Production Controller  Ros Napper
Project Editor  Lin Clements
Photographer  Simon Whitmore

Visit our website at www.davidandcharles.co.uk

David & Charles books are available from all good bookshops; alternatively you can
contact our Orderline on (0)1626 334555 or write to us at FREEPOST EX2 110,
David & Charles Direct, Newton Abbot, TQ12 4ZZ (no stamp required UK mainland).

# Contents

Intro

# duction

**Of all the fashion accessories**, the bag is probably the most important prop in our busy lives and very few of us are content with only one. We need a bag in every shape and size to see us through the day – from copious work bags for the office or shopping to tiny frivolous, decorative bags and purses for the evening.

The designs in this book reflect our love of bags of all kinds, and while there is a wide variety of styles and shapes to choose from, the emphasis on each bag is the beads. Whatever your level of expertise, age or style, there is a beautiful beaded bag here to suit. There are practical bags to see you through the day, like a crochet shopper or an embellished shoulder bag, where a shop-bought bag is decorated with beaded flower motifs; there are classically shaped bags such as a little red blanket bag and tasselled suede bag, ideal for a lunch date, and there are beautiful bags encrusted with beads for

evening, weddings and other special occasions. Each bag project also features a smaller accessory or variation, including a notebook cover, handbag mirror, beaded pumps and even an exquisite bridal tiara!

Clear step-by-step instructions and detailed photographs guide you through every project. If you are an experienced crafter you could choose your own colour of beads and materials to make a truly unique bag. For those with less confidence, the exact beads used and their suppliers are listed on pages 118 and 119.

In the modern world of mass production it is a pleasure to be able to make something that is quite unique while still retaining a contemporary look. Making your own bags has lots of advantages – not only the enjoyment of the making but also the choice of colour, material and beads to suit your particular outfit or style. With so many different bags to choose from you'll be kept busy for a long time to come.

# Equipment

Making beaded bags requires little specialist equipment – you will probably already have most of the items listed here. If not, all materials and equipment used in the book are readily available from craft or jewellery suppliers. If you don't have a local shop, check the supplier's list on page 119 to find companies who operate mail order or websites.

## Needles

When sewing, choose a needle that matches the thickness of the thread you are using so the thread passes easily through the fabric. When attaching beads, check that the beads will pass over the eye of the needle before beginning. Often a fine sewing needle is all that is needed for sewing even the small delicas and seed beads but a beading needle is easier to use when working bead stitches and when netting.

Beading needles are longer than normal sewing needles with a flat eye that can pass through the small holes in seed beads. The two most common sizes used are 10 and 13. Size 10 is a good standard needle but if you are going to pass the needle through a bead several times you will need to use the finer size 13. Beading needles can bend or break easily so make sure you have a good supply of both sizes available.

Some of the projects use a bodkin. This is a large blunt-ended needle which can be used to thread cord or ribbon through a casing or tube.

## Needle Threader

This little gadget is an essential tool for threading beading needles and fine sewing needles. Simply thread the fine wire loop through the eye of the needle, feed the thread through the loop and then pull gently to take the thread through the needle eye.

## Thread

It is essential to use a strong thread when attaching beads to bags so they do not come adrift when the bag is in use. A double length of polyester sewing thread is ideal for couching or embroidery techniques but stronger threads such as coton perlé can be used for larger beads. Quilting thread or Nymo thread (a multi-filament nylon thread) are more suitable for other beading techniques such as three-bead netting.

Nymo thread is available in a range of thicknesses: the standard thickness for seed beads is D, while the finer size B is ideal when passing the thread through a bead several times. Both thicknesses of Nymo thread come in a range of colours which can be matched to your beads.

Quilting thread is a cord thread and ideal for making fringes and tassels as it allows the beads to swing attractively. As it is a round thread, flatten quilting thread at the end and cut at an angle to make it easier to thread the needle.

## Thread Conditioners

Thread conditioners strengthen and protect thread and make it less prone to tangling. It is not always necessary to condition threads when working with seed beads. On the other hand, bugle and hex beads have sharp edges and it is recommended that you condition your threads when using these beads. Run your thread through the conditioner, avoiding the needle area, and then pull the thread between your finger and thumb to remove any excess conditioner and to smooth the thread.

## Scissors

A sharp pair of embroidery scissors is useful for cutting thread to length and snipping off threads close to the beadwork. Use larger dressmaking scissors for cutting fabric and keep a separate pair of craft scissors for paper.

## Bead Mats

Use a bead mat to spread beads out while you work as this will allow you to discard any misshapen ones and pick the beads up easily on the needle. To make a bead mat, cut a piece of chamois leather or glue a square of velvet to a piece of card. The close pile on these materials prevents the beads from rolling away as you pick them up.

## Fabric Markers

Water-soluble markers and vanishing markers are both suitable for marking designs on fabric for bead embroidery. The vanishing marker disappears over several hours and is ideal when you are working on a small area or on fabric that can't be wetted. The water-soluble marker is more permanent as it won't disappear until sprayed lightly with water.

## Fabric Glue

Fabric glues should remain pliable once they are dry so that the feel of the fabric is not too different. Glues that stick once they have become tacky are generally the most suitable for fabric. Spread a thin layer of glue on both pieces of fabric and then press together.

## Knitting Needles

The size of knitting needle you choose depends on the thickness of the yarn and the size of stitches required. Knitting yarns have the recommended needle size printed on the label: you will need to experiment to find the ideal needle for other yarns. Ask at your local wool shop for fine, double-ended needles or try mail order (see Suppliers, page 119).

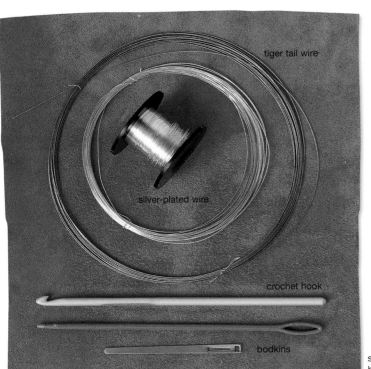

knitting needles

tiger tail wire

silver-plated wire

crochet hook

bodkins

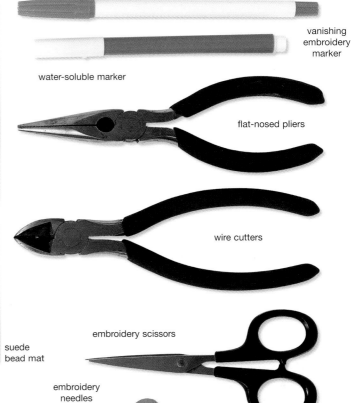

vanishing embroidery marker

water-soluble marker

flat-nosed pliers

wire cutters

embroidery scissors

suede bead mat

embroidery needles

thread conditioner

needle threader

quilting thread

beading needles

sewing thread

Nymo thread

## Crochet Hooks

Crochet hooks are available in a range of sizes. British sizes are normally quoted in millimetres, with America sizes using a lettering system (a range is given in the panel below). If using knitting yarn, the recommended knitting needle size is also the correct size for the crochet hook. If the yarn doesn't have a recommended needle size, experiment by crocheting several small squares to find the best size for your yarn.

### Crochet Hook Sizes

| UK | US | UK | US |
|---|---|---|---|
| 2.25mm | B1 | 3.75mm | F5 |
| 2.75mm | C2 | 4mm | G6 |
| 3.25mm | D3 | 4.5mm | G7 |
| 3.5mm | E4 | 5mm | H8 |

## Wire

This is used in beadwork when the beads have to hold a particular shape or if the wire is part of the decorative effect – see the bridal bag on page 82 and the tiara on page 88). 

Jewellery wire is available in a wide range of colours and thicknesses, from 0.2mm (36SWG) to 1.2mm (18SWG). (Standard wire gauge or SWG is a UK thickness scale.) You will find that 0.4mm (27SWG) wire is ideal for stringing size 11 seed beads. Tiger tail is a special wire that doesn't kink but keeps a soft curve. It is ideal for necklaces and was used to attach the tassels to the suede handbag on page 52.

## Pliers and Wire Cutters

Bend wire with flat-nosed pliers or use them to pull the needle through a bead that is tightly packed with thread. Flat-nosed pliers are also useful if you have threaded too many beads on to your thread. To avoid removing all the beads from the thread, simply grasp the unwanted bead in the tip of the pliers and squeeze – you *must* cover your eyes as you do this, as the bead will shatter into tiny glass shards. Use wire cutters to remove the wire ends close to beadwork.

## Sewing Machine

The projects in this book only require a basic swing-needle sewing machine, with a zipper foot to allow you to stitch close to beads.

# Beads

Beads are available today in wonderful shapes and sizes and in such a vast range of colours, textures and materials that it would be impossible to show all the possibilities that could be used for beaded bags. The following information describes the beads used in this book.

## Buying Beads

The beads used in this book are all readily available from bead shops or from mail-order or web-based bead companies (see Suppliers on page 119 for full details).

Seed beads, cylinder beads and bugles are sold in a variety of packets, bags and tubes with no standard bead packet sizes. Fortunately the packets or containers usually have the weight of beads marked, which makes it much easier to decide how many packets of a particular colour you require. Some beads are sold in round weights such as 5g or 100g whereas others are sold with a particular number of beads and so have an odd weight such as 4.54g. Depending on the size or type of bead there are an average number of beads per gram so it is fairly easy to work out what quantity of beads you need for a certain project.

If you are going to knit or crochet with beads look out for bead strings or hanks. There are generally about 4,000 seed beads in a hank, made up of several strings. Wood beads are often sold on strings rather than as single beads, so if you are buying a larger quantity ask your supplier when you order to leave the beads on the string so they can easily be transferred to the yarn.

It is not essential to use the exact beads shown in the projects as you can easily tailor the beads used on the bags to your own taste, but if you prefer to follow the instructions exactly, all the beads used are listed on page 118.

## Bead Finishes

Combinations of different finishes produce a huge variety of beads and some beads have two or more different descriptive words that explain exactly what they look like. Once you know what these words mean you can tell exactly what you are buying.

**Transparent** beads are clear or coloured glass that allow light to pass through. Using a dark thread can alter the bead colour.

**Opaque** beads are solid colour beads that don't allow any light to pass through.

**Translucent** beads are between transparent and opaque and are also known as greasy,

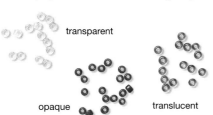

transparent

opaque

translucent

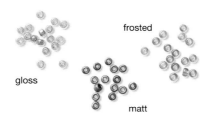

gloss

frosted

matt

opal or satin: greasy beads are made from cloudy-looking glass; opal beads are slightly more transparent; satin beads have tiny bubbles in the glass giving a directional sheen.

**Gloss** beads are very shiny, like glass.

**Matt** beads are opaque beads tumbled or dipped in acid to give them a dull, flat surface.

**Frosted** beads are clear or translucent beads that have been treated in a similar way.

**Lustre** beads have a transparent coating (coloured or clear), giving beads a subtle shine.

**Ceylon** beads have a milky, pearlized lustre.

Ceylon

**Colour-lined** (CL) beads have the hole in the bead lined with another colour. The beads can be clear or coloured.

colour-lined

metallic

**Silver-lined** (SL) beads have the hole in the bead lined with silver and look very sparkly. These beads can be bleached to remove the silver lining leaving a more subtle finish.

rainbow

**Metallic** beads include any bead that looks metallic. The finish can be painted on or, in the case of galvanized beads, electroplated to the surface. Beads with painted metallic finishes cannot be washed.

**Iris** or **rainbow** beads have been treated with metal salts to create a coating that resembles an oil slick. They are often made from dark or black opaque beads and are also known as aurora borealis (AB) beads.

# Types of Bead Used

Many different types of gorgeous beads have been used to create the bags and some are described and illustrated here.

**Seed beads** These are round donut-shaped beads ranging in size from 5 to 15. The smallest are known as petites. Larger seed beads, such as pony beads, have large holes and can be strung on to cotton yarn for knitting and crochet.

**Cylinder beads** These are precision-milled tubular beads also known by their trade names of Delicas, Antiques and Magnificas. They are ideal for bead stitches such as brick stitch as the beads sit next to one another and create an even bead fabric. They have a large hole enabling a needle and thread to be passed through each bead several times.

**Bugle beads** These are tubes of glass cut to a variety of lengths from 2–30mm (¹⁄₁₆–1¼in). The most common sizes are 4mm (³⁄₈in), 6mm (¼in), 9mm (⁵⁄₁₆in) and 15mm (⁵⁄₈in).

**Hex beads** These are like a squat bugle, made from six-sided glass cane that sparkles as it catches the light and useful for creating texture.

**Large glass beads** Crystals, teardrops and pyramids are just some of the more unusual shapes of beads available from your local bead shop. *Teardrops* are available in several sizes and have a hole at the narrow end so that they hang attractively. They can be used at the end of tassels or as droplets in bead embroidery.
*Crystals* are faceted beads that catch the light and add a touch of sparkle to your beadwork. They are available in shiny or matt finishes.
*Pyramid* beads are square beads that look like two pyramids stuck together. Their flat sides make them ideal to create circular shapes such as the rosettes on the shoe bag on page 60.

**Pearls** Pearls are satin-finished beads that add a touch of luxury to any bead project. They are available in range of colours and sizes.

**Wooden beads** Round and square wooden beads are inexpensive with a large hole in the centre ideal for threading on to wool or other yarns for knitting and crochet. Ask for the beads on a string if ordering large quantities so they can be transferred to yarn easily.

**Ceramic beads** These are a new type of bead that are also easy to thread on to thicker yarns. They come in a range of shapes and colours and add a rustic look to beadwork.

**Accent beads** These are large beads in the shape of flowers, fish and shells and are ideal for adding to ready-made bags as a decorative accent, such as the beach bag on page 28. Before using, check the bead can get wet without damaging the finish.

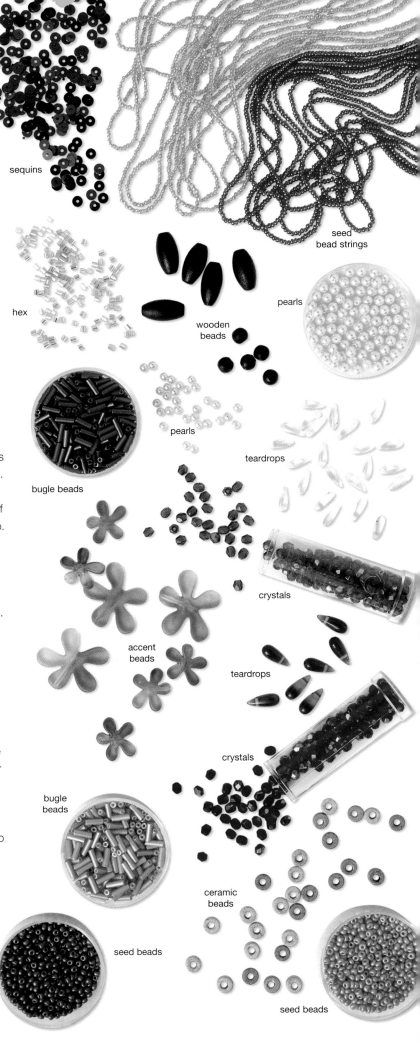

sequins

seed bead strings

hex

wooden beads

pearls

pearls

teardrops

bugle beads

crystals

accent beads

teardrops

crystals

bugle beads

ceramic beads

seed beads

seed beads

# Fabrics and fastenings

Bags can be made in a wide range of materials – from the sheerest silk organza and exquisite silk dupion to blanket fabric and leather. In this book, each bag has been specially designed with a particular fabric in mind, but it is always possible to use an alternative and the following section gives advice on choosing fabrics and fastenings.

## Choosing Fabrics

Most fabrics are suitable for making bags, however, the style of bag you choose to make will influence the type of fabric you use. For example, the tasselled suede bag on page 52 could be made in a firm fabric such as corduroy instead of leather, while the bridal bag on page 82 would be ideal for a winter wedding if made in a light silk velvet rather than silk dupion. Generally, if you want to use a different fabric to that specified in the project, choose one with similar properties and handling qualities so the bag has the same feel when finished. It is possible to change the handle of some fabrics by using interfacings. For example, if you iron a soft, heavyweight interfacing on to silk dupion you can create the lovely cylindrical shape of the bridal bag.

You should also take into consideration how the bag will be used. An evening bag for special occasions only will not need to be as hardwearing as an everyday bag. Also check that cleaning instructions for beads and fabric match. Some beads and fabrics can be hand washed, whereas others are dry-clean only.

## Silk

Silk is a luxury fabric ideal for special occasions such as weddings and black-tie events, and is available in a wide range of gorgeous colours. Depending on the effect required, choose crisp fabrics such as dupion and organza, or soft satin and silk velvet to make an extra special bag.

## Blanket Fabric

Blanket fabric has a lovely warm feel that makes it suitable for an autumn or winter bag design. Although it is a thick fabric, it is resistant to fraying and can be sewn together without making bulky seams. For best effect, use knotted blanket (buttonhole) stitch in a contrasting thread colour, as used for the little red bag on page 40.

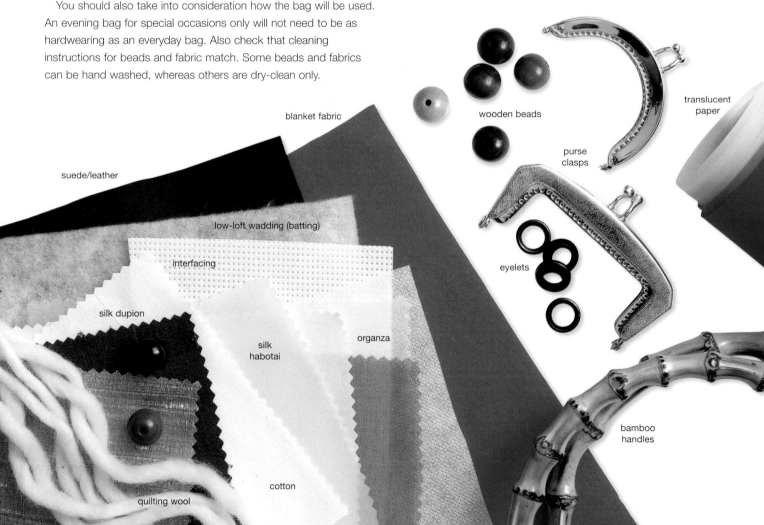

wooden beads

translucent paper

purse clasps

eyelets

blanket fabric

suede/leather

low-loft wadding (batting)

interfacing

silk dupion

silk habotai

organza

bamboo handles

cotton

quilting wool

## Leather and Suede

Leather and suede come from the same skin, the suede being the underside of the skin and the leather the top. If the skin is sold as suede the underside will be checked for defects and vice versa if the skin is sold as leather. To keep costs down ask for a skin that is in good condition on both sides and choose a lightweight leather as it will be easier to sew.

## Interfacings and Linings

Interfacings are used to stiffen fabric or create a structured shape for a bag and are usually inserted between the main fabric and the lining. Iron-on interfacings are fused to the fabric with a hot iron before making up.

There are various grades to choose from, depending on the weight of fabric being interfaced and the amount of stiffness required. For bags requiring a rigid structure, interfacings such as buckram and pelmet Vilene are ideal. Ask in your local soft furnishing store if you are unsure what to use. Choose lining fabrics that suit the weight and quality of the outer fabric. If the bag is made of silk dupion, use silk satin or habotai to line it, or if it is a heavy cotton bag, choose a firm cotton for lining.

## Paper

Bags can also be made from a variety of different papers – perfect for gift bags. Choose a paper that has a crisp feel so that the folds hold their crease and check that the paper is thick enough to support the embroidered motif and hold its shape. For a bright, modern feel, look out for the new translucent papers; these are often sold as wrapping paper but make wonderful gift bags, as seen on page 34.

## Knitting and Crochet Yarns

Cotton yarns are ideal for crocheted and knitted bags as the cotton is firm and less prone to stretching than wool yarns. You can use all sorts of cotton yarns for knitting and crochet; special crochet yarns are suitable, as is knitting cotton. You can even use an embroidery cotton like coton perlé to make tiny bags, such as the knitted pouch on page 90. When choosing a yarn, check that the beads you intend to use can be threaded on easily. If the beads are too tight, the yarn will be damaged as you push them up and down.

Knitting cottons have the size of knitting needle printed on the label, and this is generally the correct size of crochet hook to use too. When using other yarns such as embroidery cotton, a little experimentation is needed. Knit or crochet a small square to check the tension. If it's too loose, try a smaller size and if too tight, use a larger needle or hook. Knitting and crochet techniques can be found on pages 21–27.

## Handbag and Purse Clasps

You will need suitable fastenings for bag making and clasps are available in a range of sizes and shapes. Choose a plain clasp for a purse or spectacle case, or if making an evening bag select a clasp with holes for the handle. If you are looking for something really unusual, you can hunt for antique handbag clasps in markets or charity shops.

## Bag Handles

There are lots of different shapes and sizes of bag handles in a range of materials and the handle you choose will depend on the shape and size of the bag. Wood, plastic and bamboo are just some of the materials available.

## Sundries

**Wooden beads**  These are ideal for covering with seed beads to make large tassels. Choose a wooden bead that is a similar colour to the beads so it is more easily covered.

**Eyelets**  These are used to make a neat hole in fabric or leather to attach beads and tassels. Larger eyelets are sold with a special tool for fitting. See Suppliers page 119 for more unusual black eyelets.

**Quilting wool**  This is a soft bulky wool generally used in trapunto quilting. It is easy to use and ideal for padding out fabric or suede bag handles.

cotton yarn

variegated coton
perlé No 8

# Beading techniques

There are a variety of techniques used in the making of the beaded bags in this book and most of them are clearly explained within the projects. In this section you will find basic beading techniques, diagrams of the knots and embroidery stitches used, and illustrated instructions on the crochet and knitting techniques needed.

## Beginning a piece of beadwork

Work with as long a length of thread as you can comfortably sew with to reduce the number of joins – between 1–2m (1–2yd) is ideal. Nymo thread is easier to thread straight off the reel. If you are using a round thread such as a quilting thread, flatten the thread end and trim the end at an angle before threading the needle. To prevent the thread from knotting, let the needle hang loose from time to time to let it unwind. If it does coil up and loop into a knot don't panic and pull the thread tight, simply put the needle into the loop and pull gently to one side to ease the knot out.

When working bead stitches such as brick stitch or the three-bead netting used for the amulet purse on page 96, a stop bead will stabilize the first row and prevent the beads from falling off. You can use the first bead in the row or use a bead in a different colour that can be removed at a later stage.

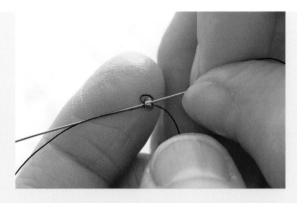

Pick up a bead and pass the needle back through the bead once or twice to anchor it. Leave a tail of at least 15cm (6in) for finishing off or adding a fastening.

## Joining on another thread

Don't work right to the end of a thread. Leave a tail of 15cm (6in) to make it easier to attach a new thread and weave the ends back into the work.

1 In closely packed beadwork, weave the new thread back and forward across the beadwork several times, bringing the new thread out through the same bead as the old thread. At a later stage, weave the old thread through the new beadwork in the same way and trim off the ends.

2 When working nets or fringes, knot the two threads together with a reef (square) knot (see opposite). Using a needle, manoeuvre the knot between two beads or to the edge of the work before you tighten it. Weave the ends into the work and trim close to the beads.

3 To finish off a thread in beadwork work one or two double half hitch knots (opposite) to secure the thread before feeding the end back through four or five beads and trimming the end. For extra security, use a drop of superglue, clear nail varnish or a product called Fray Check to secure the knot.

# Knots used in beading

There are several simple knots used in beading to anchor threads or for tying off ends securely and it is worthwhile learning these knots so that your beadwork remains intact, especially for bags that will receive much use. For extra security use a cocktail stick to drop a tiny amount of fixative such as clear nail varnish, superglue or Fray Check liquid on the knot.

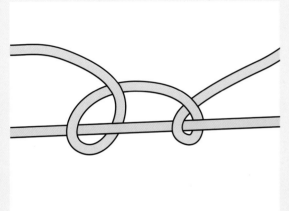

**Double half hitch** Use this knot to secure a thread in netting or fringes before feeding the end through several more beads and trimming the end.

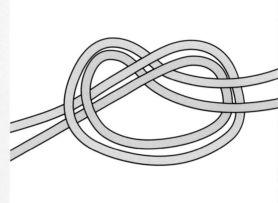

**Overhand knot** Use this to make a loop on the end of a bead string before transferring the beads on to the yarn. It can also be used to join in another thread in bead netting.

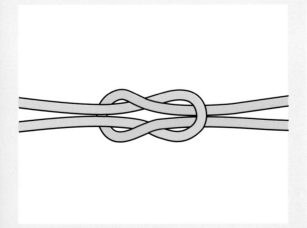

**Reef (square) knot** This is the basic knot for joining two threads of equal thickness. Feed each end back through several beads before trimming the ends.

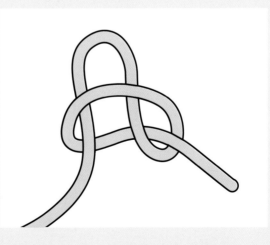

**Slip knot** This knot is used to begin a piece of knitting or crochet. Leave a tail long enough to cast on when knitting or to sew in when crocheting.

# Embroidery stitches

The following embroidery stitches have been used in some of the bags. When working embroidery use a needle that is large enough to allow the thread to pass through the fabric without leaving an obvious hole in the fabric.

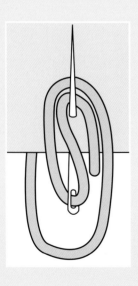

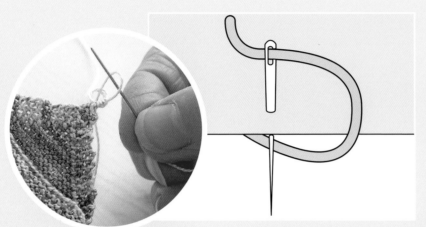

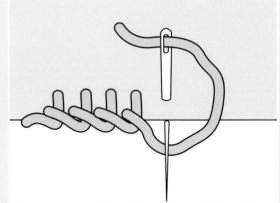

**Blanket stitch** This simple stitch (sometimes called buttonhole stitch) is used in the knitted pouch on page 90 to cover several threads to make a loop for a button or toggle fastening.

Follow the diagrams above, bringing the needle out at the edge of the fabric or thread loop. Take a stitch into the fabric or behind the thread loop and bring the needle out over the working thread. Continue making stitches in this way until you reach the end of the fabric or the thread loop is covered.

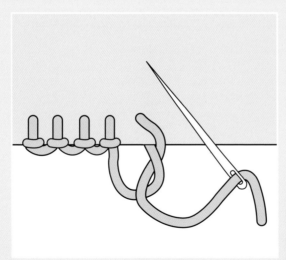

### Knotted blanket stitch

This stitch is a more secure variation of blanket stitch where the thread is wound around the needle to form a knot at the fabric edge.

Follow the diagrams left, bringing the needle out between the two layers of fabric and making a 6mm (¼in) stitch through both layers. Wrap the thread over and behind the point of the needle and pull the needle through to form a knot at the edge of the fabric. Make another stitch 6mm (¼in) further along and repeat the process.

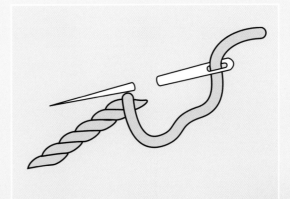

**Split stitch** This stitch is ideal for creating long, narrow lines for flower stems and it can be worked in a straight line or in a curve, as seen on the tote bag on page 46.

First make a 6mm (¼in) straight stitch. Now follow the diagram above, bringing the needle back out halfway along the stitch, splitting the thread before making another straight stitch.

**Stem stitch** As its name implies, this simple stitch is often used in embroidery to create the stems of plants and it has been used in the notebook accessory on page 44.

Follow the diagram above, first working a 6mm (¼in) straight stitch and then bringing the needle back out 3mm (⅛in) from where the thread emerges. Holding the thread loop to one side, pull the needle through. Continue making 6mm (¼in) straight stitches, bringing the needle out on the same side of the fabric each time.

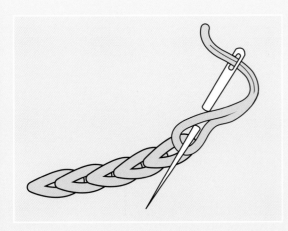

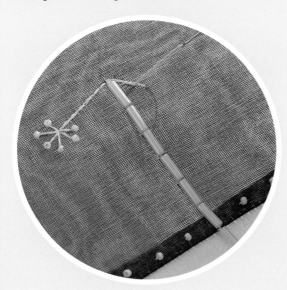

# Bead stitches

Bead stitches are a way of sewing beads together to create a beaded fabric. There are lots of different stitches that can be used to make a wide range of textures, each with distinct characteristics. Where a variation of a bead stitch has been used in the project, clear instructions for the basic technique are given here.

## Brick stitch

Brick stitch is one of the easiest stitches to work and is so called because it looks like a brick wall. Brick stitch is flexible crossways but rather stiff lengthways and can be worked flat or in a tube. It is often used to make tiny bags. A variation of brick stitch has been used to make the bead rosettes for the ribbon shoe bag on page 60.

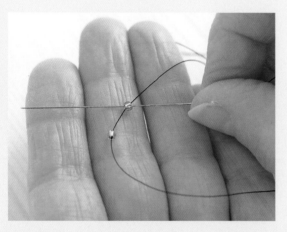

1 To make the foundation row, pick up 2 beads and pass the needle back through the first bead and then through the second bead again. Don't pull the thread too tight, so the beads sit side by side rather than one on top of the other.

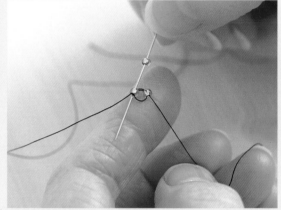

2 Pick up a third bead and pass the needle through the previous bead and back through the one just added. Continue adding beads in this way until the foundation row is the required length.

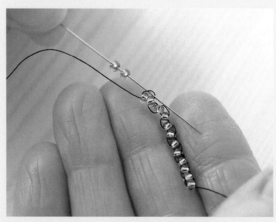

3 For the first row of brick stitch, pick up 2 beads and pass the needle under the first loop of thread joining the foundation row of beads. Pass the needle back through the second bead picked up.

4 Pick up another bead. Pass the needle under the next loop and back through the bead again. Continue adding a bead at a time to the end of the row. Turn the beading round and pick up 2 beads to begin the next row. Repeat steps 2 and 3 until the beadwork is the size required.

## Three-bead netting

Three-bead netting is a fairly solid fabric but more beads can be added in each loop to create a looser mesh which can be used for fringing along the bottom of a bag. To learn the technique, use two different bead colours. To start, thread a long length of beading thread with a beading needle on each end.

1 Pick up an odd number of beads, beginning with a dark bead and let them settle in the middle of the thread. * Pick up 3 light beads, a dark and a light and pass the needle through the third last dark bead.

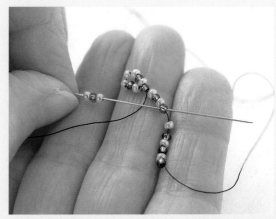

2 Pick up a light bead, a dark bead and a light bead. Miss 1 dark bead and pass the needle through the next. Continue adding 3 beads until 2 beads remain on the thread. Pick up a light and a dark bead.

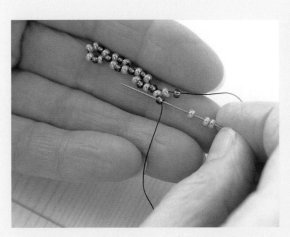

3 Put the first needle down and pick up the other. Pick up 3 light beads and pass the needle through the last dark bead added. Continue working three-bead netting to the end of the row.

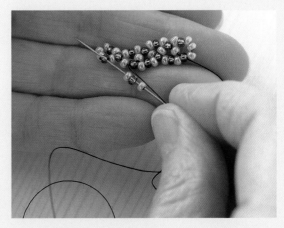

4 Using the same needle, turn and begin the two-row sequence again. Beginning at the asterisk (*), follow the instructions in steps 1–3 until the netting is the required length. Sew in the ends securely.

# Bead embroidery

Beads can be attached to most fabrics individually, in groups or in rows. It is easier to work bead embroidery if the fabric is backed with a lightweight, closely woven fabric such as cotton lawn, so threads can be anchored on the reverse side. In general, use a double length of sewing thread or one strand of a stronger thread, such as Nymo or quilting thread.

## Preparing to embroider

To prevent the fabric from puckering as you attach the beads it needs to be stretched in an embroidery hoop or supported in a fabric 'sandwich'. Choose a backing fabric that supports the main fabric without altering the way it handles too much.

1 Cut the fabric and any backing fabric at least 5cm (2in) larger all round than the finished piece. Fit the fabric into an embroidery hoop or on to a rotary frame.

2 Take two tiny backstitches on the reverse side and bring the needle out on the right side where you want the beadwork to begin.

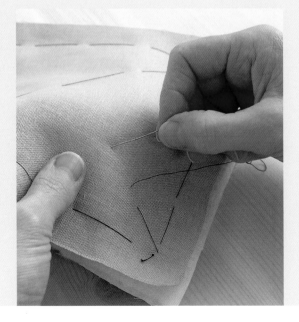

## Creating a fabric sandwich

Fitting a thin, low-loft wadding (batting) between the fabric and backing fabric provides enough body for bead embroidery and prevents the fabric from puckering. Work lines of tacking (basting) across the fabric to hold the layers together.

# Attaching beads

Beads may be attached in various ways and three common methods used in this book are sewing beads on individually, sewing on with backstitch and by couching, as follows:

## Sewing beads individually

When sewing beads individually it is essential to secure the thread carefully on the reverse side when beginning and finishing off. Use a strong thread such as quilting thread, or a double thickness of sewing cotton.

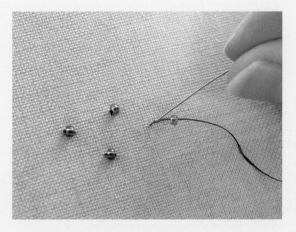

It is advisable to go through each bead twice to secure it. This makes it less likely the bead will fall off and also prevents the thread pulling through if the beads are spaced out.

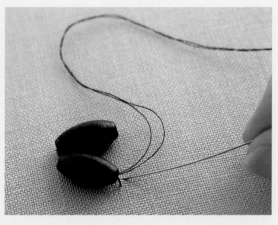

When stitching larger beads, space the two threads out in the hole so that the bead is held firmly in position. For extra security, take a tiny backstitch on the reverse side before sewing on the next bead.

## Sewing beads with backstitch

Backstitch can be used to add individual beads or several at a time. Only pick up one or two beads to follow a curved line but pick up more the straighter the line, taking the needle back through the last bead each time.

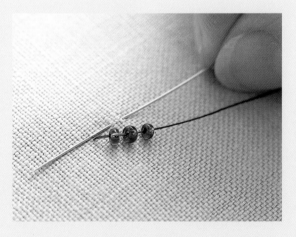

1 Pick up three beads and let them drop down to where the thread emerges. Put the needle back through the fabric at the end of the three beads. Take a small backstitch and bring the needle out between the last two beads.

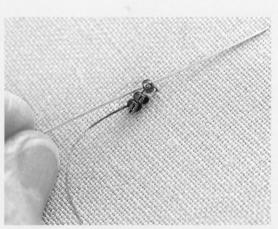

2 Put the needle back through the last bead and then pick up another three beads ready to begin again.

## Sewing beads with couching

Couching is used to apply a string of beads to fabric in a straight line or curve. You need to use two needles on separate lengths of thread – one beading needle and one sewing needle.

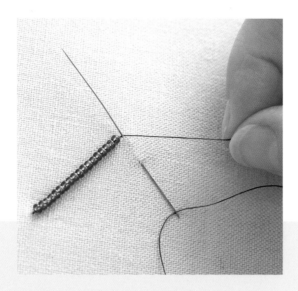

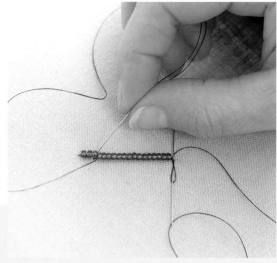

1 Bring the beading needle out where you want the beadwork to begin. Pick up sufficient beads to complete the line. If the beads are being couched in a straight line, put the beading needle in the fabric and wrap the thread around it to hold the beads taut.

2 Bring the second thread out between the first and second beads. Take the thread over the bead string and back through the fabric. Continue working down the bead strand stitching between every bead or in groups of three or four. At the end of the line take both threads to the reverse side and secure.

## Chain stitch

Chain stitch (sometimes called cable stitch) is ideal for making straps and can be embellished to make more ornate bracelets and necklaces. The number of beads can be varied in each chain to create different effects. The bead chain on the amulet purse on page 96 uses only six beads in each loop.

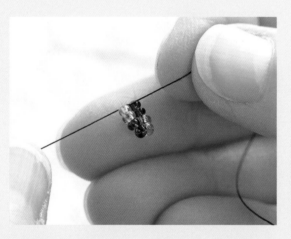

1 Pick up 2 light beads, 2 dark beads, 2 light beads and 2 dark beads. Tie the beads into a circle leaving a 15cm (6in) tail.

2 Pass the needle back through 2 dark, 2 light and 2 dark beads. Pick up 2 light, 2 dark and 2 light beads and put the needle back through the top 2 dark beads on the previous chain.

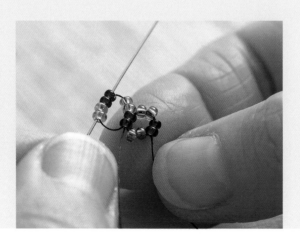

3 Pass the needle through the first 2 light and 2 dark beads just added ready to add the next chain. Continue adding 6 beads at a time until the chain is the length required.

# Knitting and crochet techniques

Knitting and crochet are attractive ways to create a beaded fabric. If you can knit or crochet it is a simple process to add the beads and if you can't now is the time to learn – it's easy! The knitted and crochet bags in this book look exquisite and are simple to make as they use only basic stitches.

## Threading beads on yarn

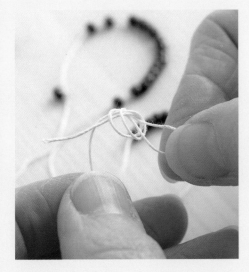

1 Separate a string of beads from the hank and tie a knot around the last bead at one end. At the other end tie an overhand knot to form a small loop (see page 13).

2 Feed the end of the yarn into the loop. Pull the beads down the string and over the overhand knot on to the thicker yarn. The beads should slip over the knot fairly easily.

3 If one of the beads is too small to slide over the knot simply squeeze the bead with pliers to break it (covering your eyes) and then continue transferring the remaining beads.

## Beginning knitting and crochet with a slip knot

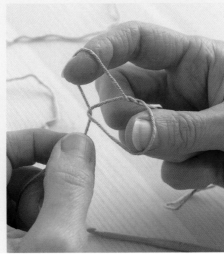

1 Hold the yarn tail in your right hand and wrap the yarn round your thumb. Take your forefinger over the top thread and under the bottom thread.

2 Lift the bottom thread and twist your finger round to catch the thread coming off the ball. Bring this thread back through between the first two threads, take your thumb out and pull gently to tighten the knot.

# Knitting techniques

The knitted pouch and purse on pages 90 and 95 use only a simple knit stitch, the only difference being the size of the needles and the fineness of the yarn. If you are accustomed to long knitting needles it takes a little while to get used to short needles, but if you haven't knitted before it is easy to learn. Start with a thicker yarn to begin with and then once you have learnt to knit you will be able to knit the little beaded bags with comparative ease. See page 24 for knitting abbreviations used.

## Casting on

There are two methods of casting on: one uses two needles and is ideal for knitting garments as the bottom edge is quite stretchy; the other method (shown here) produces a firmer edge, which is ideal for the edge of a bag.

1 Make a slip knot part of the way down the yarn, leaving a tail. Leave 1–2.5cm (½–1in) per stitch, depending on the thickness of the yarn. Fit the slip knot on the right-hand needle.

2 Wrap the yarn around your left thumb and slot the needle in the loop as shown.

3 Wrap the tail end of the yarn between thumb and needle and lift the loop over on to the needle to create the stitch. Repeat to make the required number of stitches.

## Knitting a stitch

1 Put the spare needle into the first loop and take the yarn over the lower needle.

2 Holding the yarn taut, push the needle and bring the other needle through to form a stitch.

3 Lift the stitch off the lower needle. Begin at step 1 again and continue to the end of the row.

## Making one stitch

1 Knit a stitch as normal but keep the stitch on the left-hand needle.

2 Knit into the back of the stitch on the left needle before letting it slip off on to the right needle (thus creating two stitches where there was one).

## Knitting two together

1 Insert the right-hand needle into the next two stitches from left to right.

2 Put the yarn over the needle and lift both stitches off together.

## Adding beads while knitting

1 Refer first to the project pattern for the number of beads to thread on to your yarn (see also page 21). Insert the right-hand needle into the front of the next stitch and let it slip off the left-hand needle on to the right-hand needle.

2 Bring the bead up to the knitting and knit the next stitch as normal. In the next row the slip stitch is knitted in the usual way.

## Knitting abbreviations

| | |
|---|---|
| K1 | knit 1 stitch |
| K1 row | knit 1 row |
| sl | slip a stitch |
| tog | together |

## Casting (binding) off

1 Knit the first two stitches in the row. Insert the left-hand needle into the first stitch and lift it over the second stitch and carefully off the end of the needle.

2 Continue knitting one stitch at a time, lifting the previous stitch over the one just knitted until you have cast (bound) off the whole row.

3 To finish off a piece of knitting or crochet, cut the yarn and pull the last stitch until the tail comes through the stitch. Sew in the tail or use for sewing pieces of knitting together.

# Crochet techniques

This section describes the basic crochet techniques you will need for the shopping bag on page 74 and make-up bag on page 80. The instructions are for a right-handed person. Hold the hook between finger and thumb in your right hand. Hold the tail end of the yarn between the two middle fingers and wrap around the little finger. This keeps the thread taut so the stitch can be formed. The tension is controlled by the first finger of the left hand. Please note: American terms for crochet stitches are different to those used in the UK but the instructions given below should be clear for all. See page 27 for crochet abbreviations.

## Crocheting a single chain (ch)

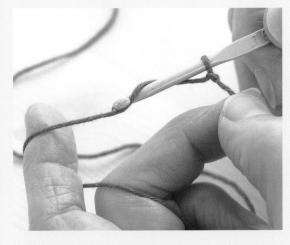

1 Make a slip knot on the end of the hook. Take the crochet hook under the yarn. (This is normally abbreviated to 'yo' or 'yoh' meaning 'yarn over hook', but in practice you move the hook under the yarn.)

2 Carefully draw the yarn through the loop on the hook to form a new loop.

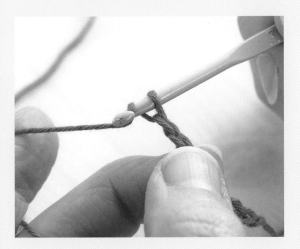

3 Repeat this process until the chain is the length that you require.

4 To make a chain into a ring, take the hook into the first chain stitch, yoh and pull the yarn through both loops on the hook to form a new loop. This is known as slip stitch (sl st).

# Double crochet (dc) *single crochet in US*

1 Skip one chain stitch, insert the hook into the top loop of the next chain stitch.

2 Yoh, draw the yarn through first loop only, yoh and draw through both loops. Repeat to the end of the row.

3 Turn and make one chain stitch, known as a turning chain. Work the next stitch under both loops of the second stitch from the hook. Continue to the end of the row.

# Treble crochet (tr) *double crochet in US*

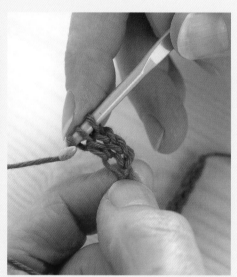

1 Skip three chain stitches, yoh, insert the hook under the top loop of the next chain stitch. Yoh, and draw the yarn through the chain only.

2 Yoh, draw the yarn through the next two loops on the hook. (The picture shows the hook being drawn through the first of the two loops.)

3 Yoh, draw the yarn through the two remaining loops on the hook. At the end of the row work three turning chain stitches and work the next treble under both loops of the second stitch from the hook. Work the last treble of the row into the third of the three turning chain stitches from the previous row.

# Crochet abbreviations

| | |
|---|---|
| yoh | yarn over hook |
| sl st | slip stitch |
| ch | single chain |
| dc | double crochet (*known as single crochet in US*) |
| tr | treble crochet (*known as treble crochet in US*) |

## Adding beads when crocheting

1 Beads can be added in a single chain or while working treble crochet (tr). Drop a bead down to the hook, then work a single chain on the other side of the bead.

2 Complete one treble (tr) and drop a bead down the hook. Work the next treble as normal, trapping the bead between the stitches.

## Finishing off crochet

To finish off a piece of crochet, cut the yarn and pull the last stitch until the tail comes through the stitch. Sew in the tail or use for sewing pieces together.

This attractive make-up bag is constructed using alternate rows of double and treble crochet – see page 80 for details.

# Flower Beach Bag

One of the easiest ways to make a beaded bag is to embellish a bag you have bought. There are lots of ways to add beads to a ready-made bag and the method you choose will depend on the bag's shape and style. As it is more difficult to add beads once the bag is complete, it is better to create the motif and attach it in one piece. The pretty flower stems on this bag are made with wire so they hold their shape and are sewn on securely with strong thread. An alternative idea, shown on page 32, uses a cotton bag 'blank' that you can dye or paint yourself and decorate with beads.

# You will need

Three large and four small peacock flower beads ● 2g each size 9 satin-finish seed beads in pink, turquoise and navy ● 2g each 6mm satin-finish bugles in pink, turquoise and navy ● Silver-plated wire 0.56mm (24SWG) ● Wire cutters and pliers ● Sewing thread and needle (See page 118 for bead details)

1 Make a stem with two leaves by first cutting a 40cm (16in) length of the silver-plated wire. Pick up a navy seed bead on the wire and bend over about 2cm (¾in) from the end to trap the bead. Feed a large peacock flower bead over the long end of the wire and feed the short end into the bead to secure the seed bead at the top.

2 Pick up 4 navy bugles and let them drop down to the flower bead. Now make the leaf shape by picking up 30 navy seed beads and dropping them down to the bugles. Bend the wire in the middle of the seed beads and holding the beaded wire between your finger and thumb, twist to form an oval below the bugle stem.

3 Pick up 3 more navy bugles followed by 22 navy seed beads. Make a smaller leaf shape by twisting the beaded wire just below the bugles as before. Pick up a further 9 navy bugles and a navy seed bead. Bend the wire over the seed bead at the end of the stem and trim the excess wire with wire cutters.

4 To create the veins on the leaves, wrap a length of silver-plated wire around a leaf shape where it joins the stem. Pick up approximately 10 seed beads to make the centre of the leaf. Wrap the wire around the top of the leaf.

5 Feed the wire down through 3 or 4 seed beads around the edge of the leaf. Pick up 3 seed beads and wrap the wire around the centre of the leaf; add another 2 seed beads and wrap the wire around the opposite edge of the leaf. Feed the wire down through 2 or 3 beads on the edge of the leaf and repeat the process until the leaf is complete then snip off the excess wire. Make a turquoise flower stem in the same way.

6 Cut a 50cm (20in) length of silver-plated wire and, using the pink beads, make the centre flower stem with two large leaves and two small leaves in a similar way to the navy flower stem. Make four shorter stems with smaller leaves and small flower beads. Use the pink beads for two of the stems and one stem in each of the other colours so that you have seven stems in total, as shown.

7 Fill a 15cm (6in) length of silver-plated wire with navy seed beads and bend the wire over at the end to secure the beads. Repeat with turquoise seed beads. Place the flower stems into position on the front of the bag. Bend the two seed bead lengths into wavy shapes and pin underneath the flower stems so they touch the wavy lines.

If possible, unpick one of the seams of the lining of the bag to make it easier to sew the stems on to the bag. You can close the seam with slipstitching after.

8 Using a sewing needle and double length of sewing thread, couch all the beaded wires on to the bag every 1–2cm (⅜–¾in) to secure.

## You will need

Bright yellow and red cold-water dyes

Cold-water dye fix

Chunky sun-shaped stamp

Easy Batik

Paintbrush

Anchor variegated coton perlé No 8 colour 1320

Embroidery needle

Washer-style ceramic beads in deep red, pink, lilac, cerise and silver

Sewing thread to match beads

# Try this...

## Cotton tote

A plain white cotton tote bag is like an artist's blank canvas and can be coloured anyway you like and then embellished with simple embroidery and beads. This bag was dyed and the design applied using a product called Easy Batik, but you could try other textile techniques such as stamping, fabric paints or tie dye.

1 Dye the cotton bag bright yellow following the manufacturer's instructions and allow to dry. Press flat and mark the centre point of the bag. Place a sheet of paper inside the bag to protect the back layer.

2 Paint the sun stamp with Easy Batik and stamp the shape at the centre point. Stamp a sun above and below this centre sun. Draw three wavy lines on either side of the sun motifs, paint a 6mm (¼in) band of Easy Batik along the lines and allow to dry overnight.

3 Press each area of the bag using a pressing cloth for two minutes to set the Easy Batik. Following the manufacturer's instructions, dye the bag with the red dye. Don't fold the bag or leave it in the dye for longer than 30 minutes.

4 Rinse the excess dye, hang the bag to dry and then press. Work running stitch around the edges of the design motifs using an embroidery needle and a single strand of coton perlé. Finish all threads securely on the reverse side and press.

5 Position the ceramic beads on the front of the bag, mixing the colours randomly for a pleasing colour spread. Mark the position of each bead lightly with a pencil.

6 Using matching sewing thread, attach the beads individually one at a time using three oversewing stitches. Secure the threads on the reverse side with tiny backstitches.

# Beaded Gift Bags

Gift bags are the ideal solution for awkward-shaped presents or tiny gifts that are too difficult to wrap – simply wrap the items in delicately coloured tissue paper and place them inside. These bags are handmade from translucent wrapping paper, which is available from most good paper craft shops, but if you are short of time you could just stitch the little beaded panel and stick it to the front of a bought bag. You can make gift bags for all occasions by changing the bead motif on the embroidered panel – see page 39 for different ideas to try.

# You will need

15cm (6in) square of silk habotai ● 15cm (6in) square of low-loft wadding (batting) ● 15cm (6in) square white cotton backing fabric ● Water-soluble fabric marker ● Swing-needle sewing machine ● Pink machine embroidery thread ● Tacking (basting) thread and pale green sewing thread ● 1g size 11 pink-lined seed beads ● 1g size 11 lime seed beads ● Beading needle ● Translucent paper 21 x 39cm (8¼ x 15½in) ● 30cm (12in) silver-plated wire 0.56mm (24SWG) ● Double-sided adhesive tape   (See page 118 for bead details)

1 To make the beaded motif, first trace the holly leaf template on page 112 directly on to the silk habotai using a water-soluble marker pen.

2 Layer the cotton backing, wadding (batting) and then the silk and pin together. Tack (baste) around the motif to secure the layers. Set your sewing machine to a narrow satin stitch and thread with pink machine embroidery thread. Machine satin stitch around all sides of the motif (see tip, left).

If you do not have a sewing machine, the edges of the silk panel can be bound with satin bias binding or finished with knotted blanket stitch.

3 Thread a beading needle with a double length of pink thread and bring out at the edge of one of the berries. Pick up about 11 pink seed beads and take the needle back through where it came out. Form the beads into a circle and couch down (see page 20) around the edge of the berry with the same needle and thread. Fill in the berry with pink beads. Create the other two berries in the same way.

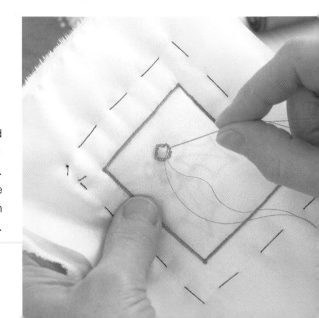

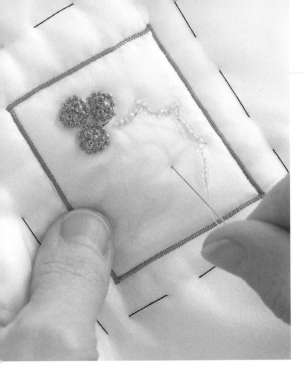

4 Thread the beading needle with a double length of pale green thread and bring out at the base of a leaf shape. Pick up sufficient lime beads to cover the first curve of the leaf and insert the needle through the fabric at the end of the curve. Couch these beads along the line. Continue around the leaf until the outline is complete.

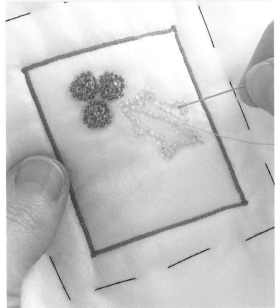

5 Couch a line of lime beads down the centre of the leaf and then fill in one side only, following the curved lines of the leaf as much as possible. Decorate the second leaf motif in the same way. Finish all threads off securely on the reverse side.

6 To make the bag, follow the diagram on page 116. Fold the sheet of translucent paper in half widthways and mark 3cm (1³⁄₁₆in) away from the centre fold on both sides. Fold the paper between the marks to create the base of the bag. Open out the paper. Mark 6cm (2⅜in) from the edge of the paper along each short end. Fold down the long edge of the paper between the marks and then fold the edge back on itself to form the sides of the bag.

7 Open out the last fold on each side. Bring one side of the bag to the vertical and fold the paper to form a neat diagonal line across the bottom. Fold up the second side to form a neat triangular flap on the inside. Open out and repeat the diagonal folds on the other side.

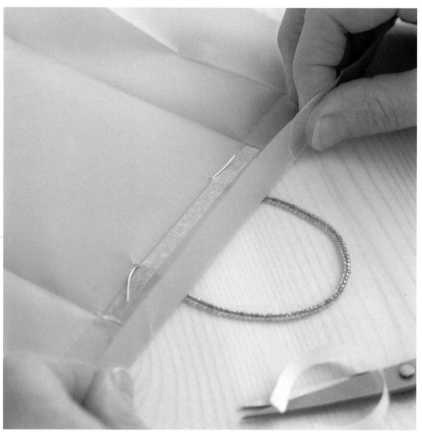

8 To make a handle, cut two 18cm (7in) lengths of wire. Bend over 1.5cm (⅝in) at one end and pick up sufficient pink beads to cover the wire, leaving 1.5cm (⅝in) free at the other end.

9 Open out the previously folded bag and fold over 2cm (¾in) along each short edge, then fold over again to form a double hem. Mark 2cm (¾in) from the edge of the front and back panels. Snip into the top folded edge with scissors to provide access for the handle. Feed the wire through the holes. Stick a piece of double-sided tape along the first fold line, secure the wire to it and then fold over the double hem. Fit the second handle to match on the back panel.

10 Fold the bag up for the final time, tucking one side into the other on the side panels. To shape the bag, crease the centre folds on the sides inwards. Trim the bead motif along the edge of the satin stitch and stick it to the front of the bag using double-sided tape.

# Try this...

## Special-occasion gift bags

You can make gift bags for any occasion by choosing a small simple motif to bead – a few hearts for Valentine's Day, a pretty flower for Mother's Day or a sweet little pram for a new baby are quick and easy ideas (templates provided on page 115). Don't despair if you don't have a sewing machine, simply sew the bead motifs on to a piece of felt and then trim the edge decoratively with pinking shears.

# Red Blanket Bag

This eye-catching bag can be made from any fabric that is resistant to fraying such as blanket fabric or heavyweight felt. The bag is easy to make as it is simply four layers of fabric stitched together with knotted blanket stitch (see page 14). This variation of blanket stitch is more secure and so is ideal for binding bag edges. Choose bead and thread colours that contrast with the fabric so that the design is bold and the stitches become a decorative feature. If you like to carry a note-book on your travels, why not make a pretty, matching cover as described on page 44?

# You will need

0.5m (½yd) wool blanket material ● Forty-five 10mm (⅜in) black wood melon beads ● Ten 6mm (¼in) black wood beads ● 35 x 70cm (14 x 28in) medium-weight interfacing (buckram) ● Black coton perlé No 5 and No 8 ● Tapestry needle  (See page 118 for bead details)

1 Enlarge the template on pages 114/115 and cut out around the solid lines. Pin the template to a double thickness of blanket fabric and cut around the outside of the template, keeping the cutting line as smooth as possible.

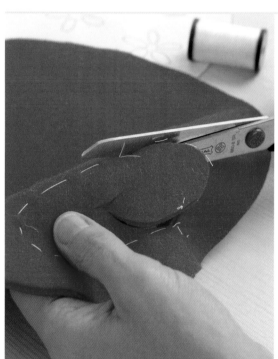

2 Tack (baste) around the handle hole to transfer the outline on to the blanket fabric. Remove the paper template and cut out the hole along the tacked line. On one piece of the blanket fabric mark the position of the flower centres with pins, using the template as a guide.

3 Using the finer coton perlé, sew 5 melon beads in a flower shape at each pin mark. To hold each bead steady, take the needle through each bead twice spreading the stitches slightly. Secure the thread on the reverse side with two tiny backstitches that don't show on the right side. Then, using the template as a guide, attach 9 or 10 round beads scattered around the flower shapes.

4 Cut a piece of interfacing the same size as the bag. Trim 6mm (¼in) from the outside edge and around the handle hole. Lay the interfacing on the plain piece of blanket fabric.

Work the blanket stitch in a stabbing motion so the stitches are the same size on the front and back of the fabric.

5 Pin the beaded fabric on top of the interfacing. Tack (baste) around the edge and the handle hole. Thread a tapestry needle with a length of No 8 coton perlé. Stitch into the bag panels and bring the needle out between the layers until the tail just disappears. Work knotted blanket stitch around the hole making the stitches about 3mm (⅛in) in length.

6 Work knotted blanket stitch around the top edge of the bag panel between the marks indicated on the template. Cut a second pair of blanket panels for the back of the bag and stitch together to the same stage. Decorative beads on the back of the bag are optional.

For extra strength, oversew the point where the bag opens on each side with coton perlé.

7 Lay the front and back of the bag together so that the handle holes match exactly. Trim 1–2mm (¹⁄₁₆in) from the two inside layers, from the edge of the blanket stitch around the bottom curve. Tack (baste) through all four layers. Work knotted blanket stitch along the remaining edge of the bag to finish.

## You will need

20 x 40cm (8 x 16in) wool blanket material

Notebook A6 size,
10.5 x 14.8cm
(4¼ x 5¾in)

A4 (US letter) sheet of paper

Rotary cutter, mat and ruler (or sharp fabric scissors)

Twenty-one 4mm (³⁄₁₆in) black wooden beads

Black coton perlé No 5 and No 8

Tapestry needle

# Accessorize with this...

## Notebook cover

The same felt or blanket fabric used for the little red bag can be used to make this stylish, removable cover that will transform a simple notebook. Use an embroidery stitch such as stem stitch to work the stems and leaves and then stitch on a few small wooden beads to complete the design.

1 Make a paper template of the shape required by tucking the paper inside the notebook so the paper protrudes by 6mm (¼in) at the top and one side. Mark the other edges and then cut the paper 6mm (¼in) larger than the notebook all round.

2 Lay the blanket fabric on the cutting mat and use a rotary cutter (or sharp scissors) to cut a piece the exact size of the paper template. Cut two strips the same depth and 5.7cm (2¼in) wide for the flaps.

3 Lay one of the flaps at the end of the large panel. Inserting a tapestry needle from the flap side, work knotted blanket stitch around the edge of the flap. Tuck the book into the flap to check the cover is the correct length and trim slightly if necessary.

4 Stitch the flap on the other end in the same way. Use a single length of thread to work knotted blanket stitch between the flaps on each side: avoid joining the thread where there is only a single fabric layer as there is nowhere to hide the ends.

5 Tuck the notebook inside the cover. Mark the bead design centrally on the front cover with a pencil using the template on page 117. Remove the notebook. Work stem stitch (see page 15) along the marked lines using No 8 coton perlé. Sew a round wood bead just above each of the stitched lines and then stitch a further 6 beads around each of the flower centres. Secure the thread ends on the inside of the cover to finish.

# Frosted Organza Tote

Step out in style with this delicate little tote bag made from contrasting tones of silk organza. A combination of appliqué, embroidery and tiny frosted beads is used to create the design on the front of the bag. To give it a professional finish, the bag is cleverly constructed using French seams so there are no raw edges inside the bag. This little bag is so easy to make that you could create several in different colourways to match your favourite outfits. Accessorize the bag with a matching handbag mirror and pouch as shown on page 51.

# You will need

30cm (12in) aubergine organza ● 30cm (12in) cream organza ● Water-soluble fabric marker

● Cream stranded cotton (floss) ● 1g ivory petite seed beads ● 1g small ivory bugle beads

● Beading needle ● Fusible bonding web ● Silicone paper (See page 118 for bead details)

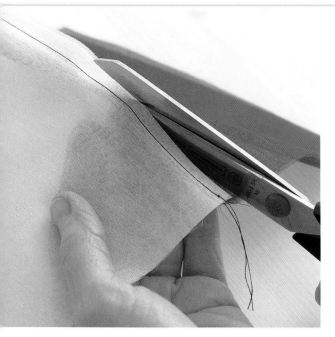

1 Cut two 16 x 20cm (6¼ x 8in) pieces from each colour of organza. Lay the two cream pieces on top of the two aubergine pieces and stitch a 1.2cm (½in) seam along one long edge. Press the seams towards the dark fabric and then trim to 6mm (¼in).

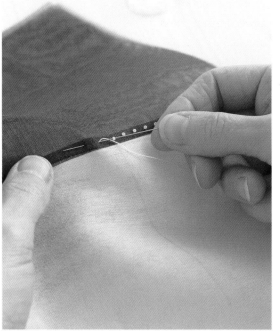

2 Lay the fabric over the template on page 113 and draw the flower stem with a water-soluble marker pen. Stitch ivory petite seed beads along the seam line, sewing one bead about 7mm (⅜in) each side of the marked stem line and about 7mm (⅜in) apart.

3 Lay a 10cm (4in) square of fusible bonding web, paper-side up, on to aubergine organza and press. Cut out six 1.2cm (½in) squares, cutting along the straight grain of the fabric wherever possible. Peel off the backing paper and position the squares, web-side down, on to the cream fabric of the bag. Leave 7mm (⅜in) each side of the marked stem line and 7mm (⅜in) between each square (see main photo on page 47). Cover the squares with silicone paper and press with a medium-hot iron to secure.

4 Tie a small knot on the end of a single strand of cream cotton (floss). Bring the needle out in the centre of the first square and make a 6mm (¼in) stitch. Bring the needle out two to three threads away from the end of the stitch and pick up an ivory petite seed bead. Take the needle back through the fabric and out again in the centre of the flower. Repeat, making seven long stitches in all to create a tiny spiky flower. Stitch a flower in each aubergine square.

5 Secure two matching threads at the bottom of the marked stem line, bringing one to the right side. Pick up enough small ivory bugle beads to fit along the stem line. Couch in between each bead using the second thread (see page 20). Sew the ends in securely at the top of the stem.

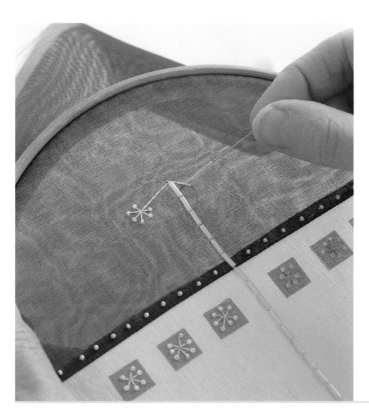

When creating the spiky flowers, sew the thread ends in at the end of each line rather than taking the threads across the back of the fabric as trailing threads will show on the right side.

6 Using the template as a guide, use the cream stranded cotton (floss) to stitch nine lines radiating out from the end of the stem in split stitch (see page 15) adding a little spiky flower at the end of each line, as in step 4.

7 To make two straps for handles, cut two 4 x 30cm (1½ x 12in) strips of aubergine organza. Press in half lengthways, fold the edges into the centre and press again. Stitch down each side very close to the edge in matching sewing thread. Trim each strap to 25cm (10in).

8 Following step 1 on page 48, make a second panel for the back of the bag.

Pin the strap handles to the top edge of each panel with the loop facing down. Cut two 18 x 23cm (7 x 9in) pieces of cream organza for the lining. Lay over the handles, matching the raw edges and stitch the seam. Press the seam open and trim to 6mm (¼in).

9 Trim the bag panels the exact size of the lining. Fold the lining to the reverse side and press the top fold. Pin the two bag panels together with right sides facing out and then stitch around the edge with 7mm (⅜in) seams.

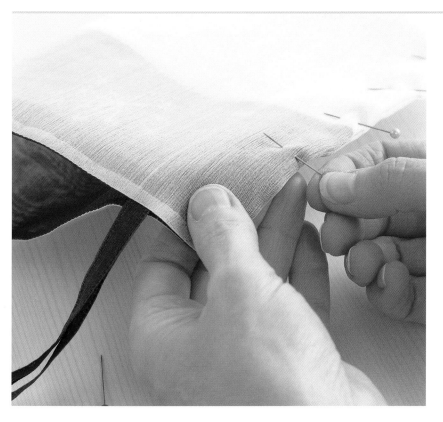

**10** Trim the seams to 3mm (⅛in) and turn the bag inside out. Ease out the corners and press the seams flat. Stitch again 6mm (¼in) from the edge and turn through to the right side. Give the bag a careful final press.

It is essential to trim the first seam carefully so that it will be completely enclosed when you stitch the second seam.

# Accessorize with this...

## Handbag mirror

Make a little pouch for a handbag mirror using the same pretty motifs and fabric as the organza tote. For an eye-catching contrast, create a spiky flower in aubergine threads and beads on cream fabric. Make the stylish pouch using the same technique as the bag. Handbag mirrors such as this are available from good needlecraft shops. They are generally sold for cross stitch projects and have instructions on how to mount your chosen design.

# Tasselled Suede Handbag

This simple little handbag is made from fine leather, shiny on one side and suede on the other and can be stitched in an ordinary sewing machine. The two textures of the leather have been used to show off the shiny black-beaded tassels that hang from the eyelet on the leather band. Keep the suede handles plain for a day bag or wrap them with shiny seed beads and bugles for a more formal evening look. To complete the set, make a slightly larger tassel in a contrasting colour and tie to a bunch of keys with a gorgeous organza ribbon.

# You will need

½m (½yd) square black leather/suede skin ● Sewing machine ● 2m (2¼yd) quilting wool ● High-tack fabric glue ● Hammer ● 6g size 11 black seed beads ● Black bugle beads: 200 (6g) 7mm, fifty 10mm and fifty 1.5mm ● Two 1.5mm black wood beads ● Black quilting thread ● Bodkin and beading needle ● 1.5mm black eyelet ● 25cm (10in) tiger tail wire (See page 118 for bead details)

1 Trace and cut out the paper template on page 116 for the main bag piece and use this to cut two shapes from the suede side of the leather. Draw along the edges with a felt pen. Cut four 4 x 20cm (1⅝ x 8in) leather strips for the bag bands and two 3 x 33cm (1¼ x 13in) suede strips for the handles.

Most skins are checked for either the suede or the leather side, so ask for a leather skin with a suede back that is even-coloured and in good condition.

2 Thread your sewing machine with black quilting thread in the top and sewing thread in the bobbin. Tighten the top tension slightly and using a long stitch, sew along the top edge of each bag panel 6mm (¼in) from the edge. Pull the quilting thread (shown in purple here for clarity) from both ends to gather the top edge until it is 20cm (8in) wide.

If you have them in your workbox, use a rotary cutter and quilting rule to cut the strips of leather accurately.

3 Lay a leather band across the top of the front gathered bag panel, with the suede side facing up, and hold in place with paper clips. Change the top thread to sewing thread, correct the tension and stitch along the top edge with a 7mm (⅜in) seam, removing the paper clips as you go. Stitch the back panel in the same way.

A roller foot suitable for sewing leather, although not essential, makes it easier to feed the thicker layers of leather through the machine when topstitching the bag.

4 To make the handles, fold the handle strips in half, suede outside. Leaving the strap open 1.2cm (½in) at each end, stitch down the cut edge. Reverse stitch at each end to secure. Cut four 48cm (19in) lengths of quilting wool, thread on to a bodkin to make eight lengths and feed the wool through one of the straps. Stuff the other strap in the same way. Trim the wool close to the end of the stitched seam.

5 Use paper clips to secure the handles to the leather band. Lay another band on top, with leather sides together, and use paper clips to hold in place. Stitch along the top edge with a 7mm (⅜in) seam, removing the paper clips as you go. Complete the back of the bag in the same way. Apply a thin layer of high-tack glue along the inside of the seam allowances and stick down.

6 Paper clip the two panels together, matching the seams and then stitch around the edge with a 7mm (⅜in) seam, removing the paper clips as you go. Trim the curved edge to 3mm (⅛in) and notch the curves, then turn through.

7 Hammer the seam allowances inside the top band to flatten them. Trim the side seam allowances if necessary and fold the band to the inside. Top stitch along the fold and again along the lower edge of the band so that the inner band is secured.

8 Bring a long length of quilting thread out at the edge of the handle seam, close to the bag band. Pick up 2 black seed beads and 1 small black bugle, and repeat four times. Wrap the beads around the handle and thread the needle through the seam about 2.5cm (1in) further up the seam from where it first emerged. Continue along the handle adding the same sequence of beads in a spiral. Space the beads by measuring and inserting pins along the seam.

9 Mark the position of the eyelet on the front of the bag. Cut the hole and insert the eyelet following the manufacturer's instructions.

10 To make a tassel, tie a length of quilting thread through the hole in a black wooden bead. Pick up 13 seed beads and take the beading needle back through the hole so the beads lie on the outside. Continue picking up 13 seed beads at a time until the bead is covered.

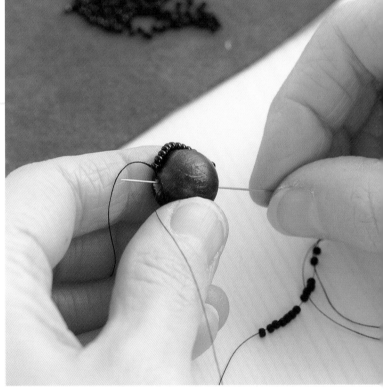

11 To fill in the gaps, pick up 9 seed beads at a time and fit between every third row of beads. Finally, fill in with 5 beads a few times until the bead is completely covered. Tie off thread ends.

12 To make the first strand of the tassel, cut another length of quilting thread, pick up 2 seed beads and 1 small bugle, twice, 2 seed beads and 1 medium bugle and then 2 seed beads and 1 large bugle. Pick up 2 more seed beads and then take the needle back through the second seed bead and the previous beads threaded. Repeat the process to make about fourteen strands in total (this can be in two groups of seven).

13 Loop the thread end between each strand to secure in one bundle. Thread the ends through the covered bead and tie off to secure.

14 Join on another length of quilting thread. Add further strands to the tassel by picking up the same sequence of beads as in step 12 and taking the needle behind the beads on the tassel head. Continue adding single strands in this way until there are about twenty-five strands. Make a second tassel in the same way.

**15** Tie off all thread ends, thread them into a large needle and sew back down through the bead hole. Tie a knot in the end of a 25cm (10in) length of tiger tail wire and feed the other end into the first tassel head from below. Pick up seed beads until the string is 15cm (6in) long. Feed the end of the tiger tail down through the second tassel head and secure underneath with a knot.

**16** Fold the tassel loop in half and feed through the eyelet. Push the tassels one at a time, through the loop to hang down the front of the bag.

# Accessorize with this...

## Elegant tassel

Make this stylish tasselled key-ring to hold your keys together. Use a larger natural-coloured bead for the tassel head and cover in a similar way to the bag tassels above, adding sufficient seed beads to cover the wooden bead and making the strands slightly longer to balance the larger bead. For each strand, pick up the following beads, repeating the sequence to the length required: 2 seed beads, 1 small bugle, twice, then 2 seed beads, 1 medium bugle, twice, 2 seed beads, 1 large bugle and 2 seed beads. Tie off all the thread ends as before and then attach a piece of organza ribbon to the top of the tassel and tie on to a key.

# Ribbon Shoe Bag

Sometimes shoes are just too special to store in the bottom of the wardrobe, and if they are only worn once or twice a year they may need a little more care to prevent them getting damaged. This gorgeous velvet bag is just the job as it can be hung from a hook or stored on a shelf, protecting the shoes inside from dust and knocks. You can use any ribbon to weave the bag, though velvet does add a touch of luxury. Make some exquisite little rosette motifs to decorate the bag and, if you fancy, add some to a pair of plain suede pumps for instant glamour (see page 66).

# You will need

15.5m (16¾yd) of 36mm (1⅜in) wide orchid velvet ribbon ● 60 x 48cm (24 x 19in) ivory lining fabric
● Fifty pale pink pyramid crystals ● 5g size 9 aubergine seed beads ● Brown quilting and sewing thread
● Beading needle and bodkin ● 50cm (20in) 7mm (⁵⁄₁₆in) aubergine satin ribbon  (See page 118 for bead details)

1 To make a beaded rosette, thread a beading
needle with a 1m (1¼yd) length of quilting
thread. Take the needle through a pyramid crystal
leaving a tail of 8cm (3in). Take the needle back
through the crystal twice to leave two threads lying
on top of one another. Repeat this process on the
opposite side of the bead.

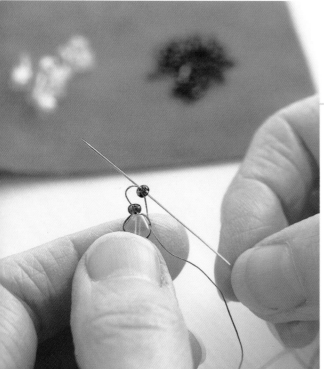

2 Work brick stitch (see page 16) around the pyramid bead as follows:
pick up 2 seed beads, take the needle under the double thread on one
side of the pyramid bead and back through the second seed bead added. Pick up
another seed bead, feed the needle under the double thread and through the seed
bead again. Continue adding beads one at a time until you reach the first bead.

3 'Tie' the last and
first beads
together by feeding the
needle through the first
bead added and back
through the last
seed bead.

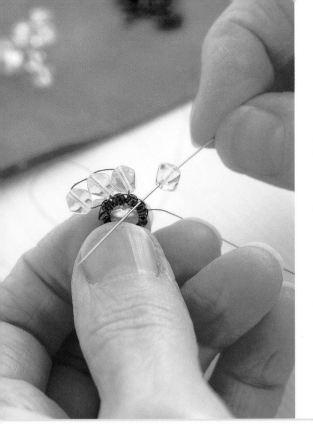

4 Pick up 2 pyramid beads and feed the needle under the second thread loop from the last seed bead added. Take the needle back through the second pyramid bead. Continue adding pyramids one at a time until you reach the first bead and then tie the first and last beads together as before. As there are fewer pyramids than seed beads you will not need to use every loop.

Don't pull the thread too tight when adding the pyramid beads as they need to fan out around the centre like flower petals.

5 The last round of beads creates a picot edge. Pick up a seed bead, take the needle under the loop of thread and back through the bead. Pick up 2 seed beads, take the needle under the loop of thread and back through the second bead. Continue adding 2 beads until you reach the first bead again. 'Tie' the beads together and add a bead to finish the picot edge. Tie off the thread end with a double half hitch knot (see page 13) and sew in the ends. Make four more rosettes in the same way.

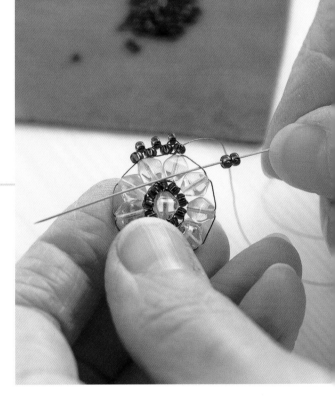

6 To make the bag, first cut fourteen 54cm (21¼in) lengths of ribbon and twenty-four 32cm (12½in) lengths. Lay seven of the longer lengths side by side on a work surface. Weave the shorter lengths across the longer lengths, beginning 1.2cm (½in) from the bottom end and leaving about 8cm (3in) of the longer ribbons free at the top edge.

7 Pin the ribbons in place and check that the panel is square and that each side is the same length. Sew the ribbons together with several tiny stitches at each point where they cross. Pick up a seed bead and sew in place with the last stitch. Leave the outside edge of the panel free of beads.

8 To line the bag, cut two 30 x 48cm (12 x 19in) pieces of lining fabric. Tack (baste) one piece along the top edge of each of the ribbon panels. Stitch a seam slightly above the top horizontal ribbon, then remove the tacking (basting) thread.

9 Pin and tack (baste) the panels together with right sides facing and seams matching. Measure and mark the lining to ensure that you stitch it the same size as the bag panels.

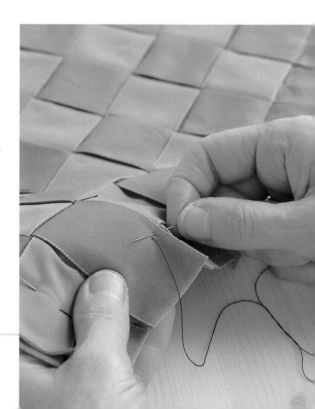

10 Velvet ribbon is prone to creep if it is not held securely before machine stitching, so tack (baste) along the edge of the ribbon panel carefully. Beginning on one side of the lining, stitch around the edge of the bag and finish on the lining, leaving a gap in the side seam for turning.

**11** Trim the seams and across the corners and turn through. Slipstitch the gap in the lining. Press the top edge and tack (baste) to hold in place. To make the casing, sew two rows of machine stitching 7mm (⁵⁄₁₆in) apart in the centre of the second horizontal ribbon down from the top edge.

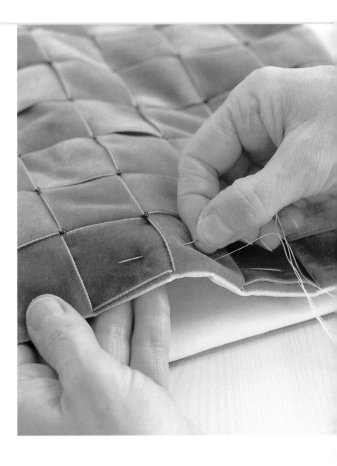

**12** Using matching sewing thread, sew the rosettes across the front of the bag. Snip into the seam between the casing lines. Thread a 50cm (20in) length of narrow satin ribbon on to a bodkin and feed though the casing and back out the same side. Feed another length through from the other side.

**13** Make two small bead rosettes (see step 3 of the beaded pumps overleaf) and thread one on to each ribbon. Tie the ends of the ribbons together and pull through the casing of the bag so the knots are at the opposite side seam. Sew the ribbon on both sides to secure the little rosettes.

# You will need

# Accessorize with these...

## Beaded pumps

Transform a pair of simple suede shoes with pretty bead rosettes — one large, one medium and one small.

1 Make a large bead rosette as described in steps 1–5 on pages 62–63.

2 To make a medium rosette, take the thread through a seed bead twice on either side as described in step 1 on page 62, then add a row of 5 pyramid beads and finish with the final picot edge as in step 5 on page 63.

3 To make a small rosette, take the thread through a pyramid bead twice on either side as described in step 1 on page 62, then work the final picot edge using seed beads as in step 5 on page 63.

4 Sew the bead rosettes to the front of the shoes using a strong quilting or Nymo thread (see tip, below). If you find it difficult to pull the needle through the fabric of the shoes, use a pair of flat-nosed pliers for extra grip.

Try on your shoes and arrange the rosettes in several ways before deciding exactly where to stitch them.

# Luxury Lattice Purse

The beads on this bag were matched to the two thread colours that make up the gorgeous silk dupion and so contrast with the fabric while still toning in exactly. You can use this method of choosing bead colours for any colour of silk that you buy; it removes much of the guesswork and ensures the colours all work together. The lattice design, worked in right-angle weave, will only fit on the bag if you use size 9 seed beads: if you use different beads make the lattice first, then measure it to find out what size of bag to make. The glasses case shown on page 73 would make an eye-catching accessory.

# You will need

33 x 40cm (13 x 16in) mauve two-tone silk dupion ● 33 x 38cm (13 x 15in) mint-green metallic organza ● 10g each size 9 seed beads in aqua, mauve and rainbow ● 200 each 4mm (³⁄₁₆in) crystal faceted beads in dark aqua and mauve ● Mauve quilting thread ● Sewing needle and beading needle  (See page 118 for bead details)

1 Cut two 15 x 19cm (6 x 7½in) pieces of silk dupion and two 15 x 18cm (6 x 7in) pieces in metallic organza. Lay a piece of organza on each piece of silk and stitch a 6mm (¼in) seam along the top edges. Press seams open.

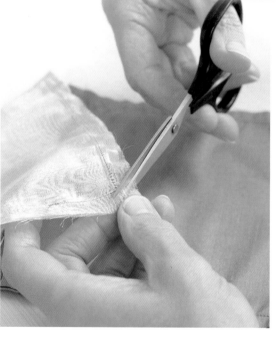

2 With right sides together, pin the two panels together, matching the seams carefully. Machine stitch (or backstitch by hand) a 6mm (¼in) seam around the panel, leaving a gap along the bottom edge of the organza for turning. Trim across the corners and turn through. Slipstitch the gap in the lining, tuck inside the bag and press flat.

3 To work the bead fringe along the bottom edge, secure a length of quilting thread at one corner of the bag. Pick up 8 mauve seed beads, 1 rainbow seed bead, 1 dark aqua faceted bead and 1 rainbow seed bead. Miss the last rainbow seed bead and take the needle back up through the other beads. Slip the needle along the edge of the bag about 4mm (³⁄₁₆in) and bring it out for the next strand of the fringe. Pick up the same beads as before but change to a mauve faceted bead. Continue along the edge of the bag, alternating the colour of the faceted beads each strand.

4 Work the right-angle weave to create the lattice beadwork for the bag front as follows: thread a fine needle with a long length of quilting thread and pick up beads in this order: 1 aqua faceted, 1 aqua seed, 2 rainbow seed beads, 1 mauve seed, 1 mauve faceted, 1 mauve seed, 2 rainbow seed beads, 1 aqua seed. Repeat this sequence and then tie the beads in a circle leaving a 15cm (6in) tail.

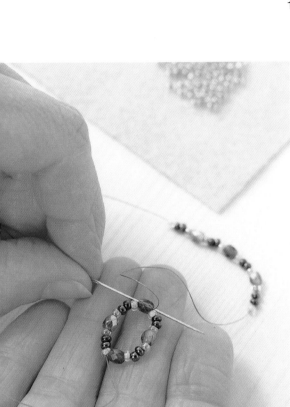

5 Feed the needle back through the beads around one side of the circle to emerge the other side of the opposite aqua bead. Pick up beads for the next circle by missing the first aqua bead in the list at step 4. Feed the needle back through the top aqua faceted bead on the last circle and then through other beads to emerge at the top of the next circle. Repeat this process until there are twelve circles in a column.

6 Tie off the thread ends with double half hitch knots (see page 13). Begin with a new length of thread. Pick up 1 aqua faceted, 1 aqua seed, 2 rainbow seed and 1 mauve seed. Feed the needle through the mauve faceted bead on the bottom circle of the first column. Pick up the remaining beads as before (step 4) to complete the circle. Feed the needle through the beads to come out at the top of the circle again.

7 Pick up beads to make the next circle round to the last mauve faceted bead. Feed the needle through the mauve faceted bead from the first column and then pick up 1 mauve seed, 2 rainbow seed and 1 aqua seed. Feed the needle through the aqua faceted bead at the top of the previous circle and then continue through the beads to the top of the circle.

8 Continue adding circles in this way to the top of the second column. Sew in the thread ends securely and use a new length of thread for each of the following eight columns.

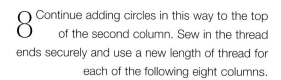

9 Lay the beaded lattice on the front of the bag and pin in place. Slipstitch along the edge of the bag, working a backstitch twice through each faceted bead. Work around the bag one side at a time.

10 To hold the bead lattice in place against the bag, work running stitch in a line up the centre row of faceted beads. Stitch into the fabric, bringing it out just in front of the bead, then slip the needle through the bead and into the fabric on the other side. Finish off the thread with two double half hitches and feed the thread end through the beads before trimming off. Repeat on the middle column of faceted beads each side of the centre line.

11 To make a 51cm (20in) strap cut four 81cm (32in) lengths of quilting thread and feed through the eye of a fine needle. Tie a knot 15cm (6in) from the end. Pick up 1 rainbow seed, 1 aqua faceted, 1 rainbow seed and 1 mauve faceted. Continue this sequence until the strap is the length required. Tie a knot at the other end to secure the beads. Sew the ends into the sides of the bag in pairs to secure the strap.

# Accessorize with this...

## Glasses case

Right-angle weave is a versatile bead stitch that can be used to create a variety of different bead lattices to decorate ready-made accessories. Choose a selection of toning seed beads and pretty, decorative beads, such as these delightful silver flower beads to transform a plain glasses case. Try out a small sample, as you will need to add fewer seed beads either side of a larger bead to keep the lattice even. Once you've worked the lattice beadwork to the same size as the item simply slipstitch it in place.

# Crochet Shopper

Most of us can remember watching our mother or grandmother crocheting bright multicoloured squares to make into blankets or cushions during the long winter evenings, and, if lucky, learnt to crochet a square or two ourselves. This practical and extremely stylish shopper is made with these same simple squares, which have been embellished with bright wooden beads and finished off with a pair of stunning bamboo handles. Should your crochet skills need refreshing, work through the techniques on page 25 and if you are looking for a smaller project to start with, try the little crochet make-up bag on page 80.

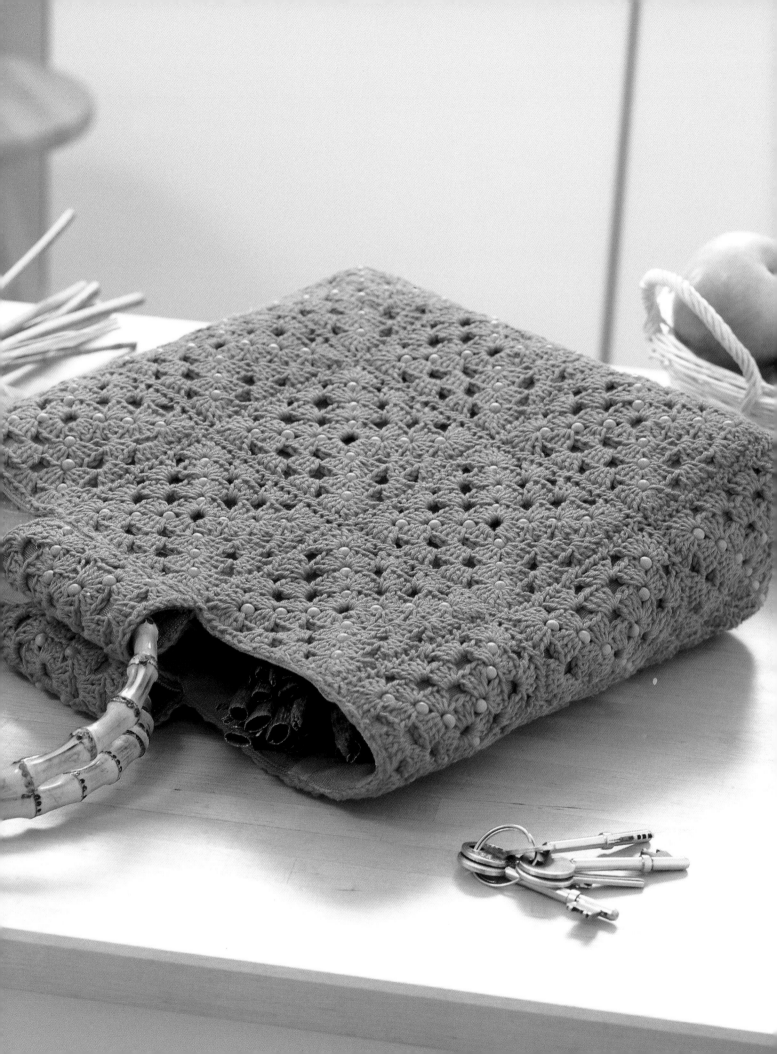

# You will need

Four balls of Rowan cotton glacé, spice 807 ● 3.5mm (US E4) crochet hook ● 348 6mm (¼in) round orange wood beads ● Tapestry needle ● 75 x 35cm (30 x 14in) interfacing (buckram or Vilene) ● 75 x 35cm (30 x 14in) lining fabric ● Two 15cm (6in) diameter bamboo handles ● Sewing machine

(See page 118 for bead details)

## Crochet Abbreviations

| yoh | yarn over hook |
|---|---|
| sl st | slip stitch |
| ch | single chain |
| dc | double crochet (*work as single crochet in US*) |
| tr | treble crochet (*work as double crochet in US*) |

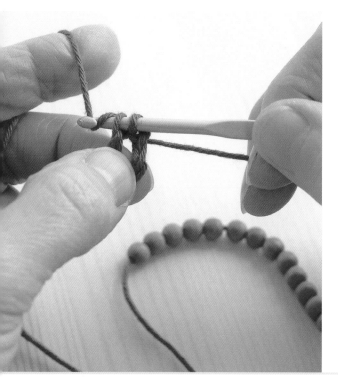

1 Transfer 12 beads on to the knitting yarn (see page 21). Attach the yarn to the crochet hook with a slip knot (see page 21) and work 6 chain stitches. Make the chain into a circle using a slip stitch (sl st) – this is worked by putting the hook through the first chain, wrapping the yarn over the hook (yoh) and pulling through both stitches to join them together.

When working the crochet squares, take the hook under the stitches above the space rather than into the stitches of the previous row.

2 **1st round:** work 4 tr into the circle. Bring a bead up to the hook and work 1 ch over the top of the bead to secure it. Repeat these two steps three more times. Work 1 sl st to join the last bead to the first tr, forming a small square.

3 **2nd round:** work 4 tr under the two loops of the stitch worked across the bead on the next corner. Add a bead using 1 ch and work a further 4 tr in the same stitch. Work 1 ch. Repeat three times.

4 After the last single ch, put the hook through the third stitch from the next corner bead. Yoh and pull through both stitches to join them. **3rd round:** work 4 tr into the stitch above the next corner bead. Add a bead using 1 ch and work a further 4 tr in the same stitch. Work 1 ch and then 4 tr into the 1 chain gap. Work 1 ch. Repeat three times, making sure the last block of tr goes into the 1 chain gap. Sl st into the third stitch from the next corner bead as before.

5 **4th round:** no beads are added in this final round. Work 4 tr into the stitch above the next corner bead. Work 1 ch and then a further 4 tr in the same stitch. Work 1 ch and then 4 tr into the 1 chain gap. Work 1 ch and another 4 tr into the 1 chain gap. Work 1 ch. Repeat three times, making sure the last block of tr goes into the 1 chain gap. Miss out the last single chain and sl st into the third stitch from the corner as before. Fasten off.

6 Crochet twenty-nine squares in total. Sew in the yarn ends on the reverse side and press each square with a steam iron, easing them into shape and trying to make all the squares the same size. Place two squares right sides together and oversew the inner stitches together along the seam. Sew in the ends securely.

7 Arrange the squares so all face in the same direction and then sew them into three rows of eight, and a row of three for the base of the bag (leaving two for the handles later) – see diagram below. Sew the three rows of eight together and then sew the row of three along the bottom, one square in from one end. With the bag right side inwards, sew the vertical side seam and then sew the base in position. Press the bag before turning through.

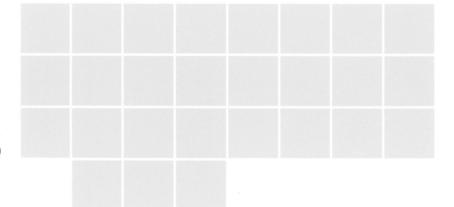

*Crochet squares layout – see step 7.*
*Each square is approximately 8cm (3in)*

8 To make the tabs for the handles, cut four 10 x 15cm (4 x 6in) pieces of lining fabric. Stitch the strips together in pairs along the long edges with 6mm (¼in) seams. Turn through and press. Cut a piece of interfacing to fit inside each panel. Pin a crochet square centrally on each fabric panel and machine stitch just inside the outside row of crochet to secure. Sew in any thread ends.

9 Cut a piece of interfacing to fit inside the bag using the layout on page 78 as a guide. Cut two pieces of lining fabric the same size and shape. Stitch the side and bottom seams to make the same box shape as the crochet. Tuck the interfacing into one of the fabric linings, fold over the top edge and tack (baste). Pin and tack the handles in the centre of each side of the bag. Machine stitch through one layer only, tuck the handles inside and tack securely.

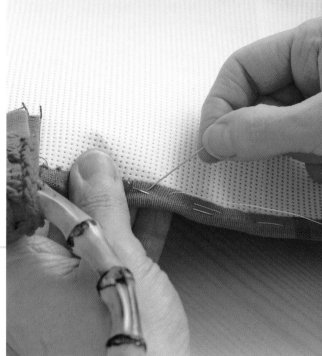

10 With the seams to the inside, tuck the lining into the bag, fold over the top edge and tack (baste). Fit the outer crochet shape over the bag and pin in position. Machine stitch through all layers, close to the top edge. You may need to hand stitch the lining across the inside of the handles as the layers will be too bulky for most sewing machines.

## You will need

One ball natural double-knitting cotton yarn

150 ceramic beads in total in deep pink, lilac, coral, pale grey and red

4.5mm (US G7) crochet hook

20 x 24cm (8 x 9½in) lining fabric

15cm (6in) off-white zip (zipper)

# Accessorize with this...

## Make-up bag

These washer-style beads slot very attractively into the treble (double) crochet but you could use any 4-6mm beads with large enough holes to feed on to the yarn. In fact, if you choose a silkier yarn the bag would be ideal for evening. Note: US crochet terms are given in brackets (parenthesis).

1 Attach the yarn to the crochet hook with a slip knot (see page 21) and work 40 chain stitches.

2 **1st row:** Put the hook into the third chain from the hook and work dc (sc) to the end.

3 **2nd row:** Work 3 ch. Yoh, put the hook in the fourth chain from the hook and work a tr (dc). Drop a bead next to the crochet hook, yoh and work the next tr (dc). Continue to the second last stitch from the end and work the last tr (dc) without a bead (24 beads in all). Repeat to the end of the row and then work 2 turning chain stitches.

4 Repeat these two rows approximately eighteen times, finishing with two dc (sc) rows. Finish off by cutting the yarn and pulling it through the last stitch. Work a second panel the same way.

5 Using a double thread and back-stitch, stitch the zip (zipper) along the top inside edge of one of the crochet panels. Stitch the second panel to the other side of the zip. Open the zip part-way, turn the crochet panels right sides together and stitch the side seams and along the bottom edge.

6 Cut and stitch a lining to fit inside the make-up bag. Turn the crochet bag right side out, tuck the lining inside and slipstitch it to the zip (zipper) tape.

## Crochet abbreviations

| | |
|---|---|
| yoh | yarn over hook |
| sl st | slip stitch |
| ch | single chain |
| dc | double crochet (*known as single crochet in US*) |
| tr | treble crochet (*known as treble crochet in US*) |

# Dreamy Bridal Bag

Weddings are the ultimate special occasion and the bride, without doubt, the centre of attention. This gorgeous little 'dorothy' bag is the ideal accessory for the bride to carry her handkerchief, lipstick and other 'bits and bobs' she might need during the day. You could make the bag using the same silk as the wedding dress and choose between gold or silver wire depending on the colour of the bride's wedding ring and other jewellery. For a finishing touch make an exquisite beaded tiara in an afternoon, using the same beading technique (see page 88).

# You will need

45cm (18in) ivory silk dupion ● 45cm (18in) ultra-soft heavyweight iron-on interfacing ● 45cm (18in) silk satin lining ● 2g each ivory and crystal seed beads ● Ten each large decorative beads: 4mm (³⁄₁₆in) crystals, pearls, teardrops and pyramid beads ● 4m (4yd) silver-plated wire 0.56mm (24swg) ● 5m (5yd) silver-plated wire 0.315mm (30swg) ● 1m (1yd) silk cord to match silk dupion ● Sewing needle and beading needle ● Ivory quilting thread ● Masking tape ● Pliers and wire cutters  (See page 118 for bead details)

1 Cut a piece of silk dupion 25 x 32cm (10 x 12½in). Cut one piece of interfacing 15 x 32cm (6 x 12½in) and another 9 x 32cm (3½ x 12½in). Iron the two pieces of interfacing, one on top of the other, along the bottom edge of the bag.

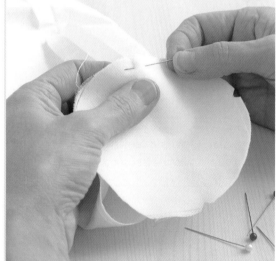

3 Make a casing by turning down the top edge of the bag by 1.2cm (½in) and then a further 5cm (2in) and press. Machine stitch a 7mm (³⁄₈in) casing 3cm (1¼in) from the top.

2 Fold the silk dupion in half widthways, right sides together, and stitch the back seam on the bag. Trim the interfacing in the seam allowance and press the seam flat. For the base, mark an 11cm (4⁵⁄₁₆in) diameter circle on silk dupion and cut two matching circles in interfacing. Iron the interfacing to the reverse side of the silk and trim off the excess silk. Mark the bottom of the bag and the base circle in quarters with small notches. Pin the circle into the bottom of the bag, matching the notches. Tack (baste) and machine stitch.

4 Cut four 45cm (18in) lengths of 0.56mm wire and twist a loop on one end of each length to stop the beads falling off. Fill two wires with ivory seed beads and two with crystal seed beads as follows: pour a small quantity of seed beads into your hand and pick them up on the end of the wire; continue until the wire is filled, twisting the wire end to secure.

5 Cut a further four 45cm (18in) lengths of 0.56mm wire and twist a small loop in the end of each. Attach a 1m (1yd) length of fine 0.315mm wire to the loop and wrap for 1.2cm (½in). Pick up 2 seed beads and a pearl on the fine wire. Drop the first seed bead down to the thicker wire and wrap to hold it in place. Secure the second seed bead a further 1.2cm (½in) along. Wrap the wire along another 1.2cm (½in) and let the pearl drop down. Fold the fine wire to make a short stem and twist the bead between the finger and thumb to secure.

6 Continue picking up 2 seed beads and a decorative bead at a time on the thicker wire and secure in place with the fine wire. Vary the length of the stems and the shape of the decorative bead to create a randomly beaded wire. Make three more similar lengths.

7 Secure the four seed bead strands to a work surface with masking tape. Plait the strands together loosely to form a fairly wide band about 32cm (12½in) long.

8 Now feed the decorative bead strands of wire one at a time in between the plaited seed strands to create a deep mesh.

9 Mark the position of the mesh on the bag with pins and then put the mesh to one side. Using a double length of matching sewing thread, sew ivory seed beads (or mixed colours) randomly all over the bag, outside the mesh panel, leaving gaps of 1–1.5cm (½–⅝in) between beads.

10 Wrap the beaded mesh around the bag and pin in position, with the ends of the wire at the back seam (see tip, above right). If necessary, remove any excess beads from the beaded wires, then twist the ends of the wires together and trim. Using matching sewing thread, sew the mesh to the bag.

11 Cut an 18 x 32cm (7 x 12½in) piece of silk satin lining and an 11cm (4⁵⁄₁₆in) diameter circle and make up as in step 2. Tuck the lining inside the bag and slipstitch to the edge of the casing. Using the point of your embroidery scissors, make a small hole at the centre front, opposite the back seam. Feed the silk cord through the casing on the bag with a bodkin, and back out the same hole.

Before wrapping the beaded mesh around the bag, roll a large piece of stiff card into a tube and fit inside the bag to hold the shape temporarily while you fit the mesh.

12 To make the tassels on the end of the cord, thread a long length of quilting thread. Fold the end of the cord over 7mm (³⁄₈in) and sew securely. Bring the needle out at the end of the cord and pick up 10 white seed beads. Pick up a small crystal teardrop and take the needle back up the seed beads and into the end of the cord. Repeat to make five strands.

To make the tassel head keep adding seed beads one at a time until the folded end of the cord is covered and the head resembles a white blackberry (see picture, above). Make another tassel on the other end of the cord.

## You will need

2g in total ivory and crystal seed beads

Five each 6mm (¼in) decorative beads: pearls, crystals, teardrops and pyramid beads

2m (2¼yd) of 0.9mm (20swg) silver-plated wire

3m (3¼yd) of 0.56mm (24swg) silver-plated wire

One reel of 0.315mm (30swg) silver-plated wire

Wire cutters and flat-nosed pliers

Masking tape

Use the 'natural' curve of the thick wire from the coil to make the curved shape of the hairband rather than trying to bend the wire to shape.

# Accessorize with this...

## Bridal tiara

This exquisite tiara is made using the same beading techniques as the decoration on the bridal bag. Simply make a thick wire hairband as a base and attach the beaded wires one at a time to create a bead-encrusted mesh. The tiara can be worn with or without a veil.

1 Cut one piece of 0.9mm (20swg) wire 45cm (18in) long and another 40cm (16in) long. Fold over the last 2cm (¾in) at each end of the longer piece to make small loops for hairgrips.

2 Hold the two pieces of wire together and wrap both at one end securely with 0.315mm (30swg) wire, covering all cut ends. Continue wrapping the wires together more openly until you reach the other end and then wrap closely to secure and tie off the fine wire.

3 Cut a 40cm (16in) length of the 0.56mm (24swg) wire. Bend over one end and fill with ivory seed beads. Mark the middle 18cm (7in) of the tiara with masking tape. Wrap the end of the beaded wire around the tiara at one mark. Make three semicircular loops with the beaded wire and then wrap the end around the tiara to secure.

4 Cut three 30cm (12in) lengths of 0.56mm (24swg) wire. Fill one with ivory seed beads and the other two with crystal seed beads. Weave and loop the beaded wires across the front of the tiara to create a bead mesh that rises up in the centre and falls off at each side.

5 Cut three 30cm (12in) lengths of 0.56mm (24swg) wire. Cover each of these wires with an assortment of beads as described on page 85, steps 5–6 of the main project.

6 Wrap and weave each of these beaded wires in turn through the bead mesh to create an attractive, balanced effect. Trim off any wire ends with wire cutters and make sure there are no sharp, jagged ends.

# Knitted Pouch

This exquisite little pouch is knitted using coton perlé. More generally used for embroidery or needlepoint, perlé comes in a wide range of colours including gorgeous multicoloured yarns that set off beads beautifully. Experienced knitters may find it slightly strange to work with such small fine needles to begin with but as the pouches are made using a simple knit stitch they are easy enough for a beginner to make. Instructions on how to knit are on pages 21–24. Buy the seed beads in a hank so that they can be transferred on to the yarn easily. Make this trendy little day purse or for your next evening out create the luxurious version shown on page 95.

# You will need

One ball of Anchor variegated No 8 coton perlé, colour 1344 ● One hank of size 11 pink-lined seed beads ● Size 0000 (1.25mm) double-pointed knitting needles ● Tiny blue button ● Tapestry needle  (See page 118 for bead details)

**1** Transfer four strings of seed beads on to the coton perlé (approximately 1,250 beads) – see page 21.

## Knitting abbreviations

| | |
|---|---|
| K1 | knit 1 stitch |
| K1 row | knit 1 row |
| sl | slip a stitch |
| tog | together |

**2** Slide the beads down the coton perlé so that there is about 1m (1¼yd) of yarn free. Use the thumb technique described on page 22 to cast on.

*Cast on 27 stitches and then knit three rows (K3 rows).*

The first row will take a little care but knitting on such thin needles gets easier by the second and third rows as the stitches loosen.

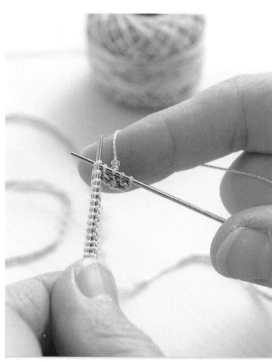

**3** To learn how to slip a stitch (sl) while adding a bead, see page 21. To add a bead, simply bring the bead up the coton perlé close to the knitting and knit the next stitch so the bead is trapped.

*K3 * sl 1, slip 1 bead, K3 – repeat from * to the end. K1 row. Repeat the last two rows twice. There will be three rows of single beads spaced across the knitting.*

*K3 * sl 1, slip 2 beads, K3 – repeat from * to the end. K1 row. Repeat the last two rows until there are three rows of double beads spaced across the knitting, with the bead side facing ready for the next row.*

4 In order to shape the bag you need to make a stitch (make 1) behind each group of beads (see page 23). Continue with the pattern, as follows:

*K3 \* make 1 on the slip stitch, K3 – repeat from \* to the end (33 stitches).*

*K3 \* sl 2, slip 3 beads, K3 – repeat from \* to the end. K1 row. Repeat the last two rows until there are three rows of three beads spaced across the knitting, with the bead side facing ready for the next row.*

*K4 \* make 1 on the next slip stitch, K4 – repeat from \* to the last three stitches, K3 (39 stitches).*

*K3 \* sl 3, slip 4 beads, K3 – repeat from \* to the end. K1 row. Repeat the last two rows until there are five rows of four beads spaced across the knitting, with the bead side facing ready for the next row.*

*K4 \* make 1 on next slip stitch, K5 – repeat from \* to last four stitches, K4 (45 stitches).*

*K3 \* sl 4, slip 5 beads, K3 – repeat from \* to the end. K1 row. Repeat the last two rows until there are five rows of five beads spaced across the knitting, with the bead side facing ready for the next row.*

5 Decrease the number of stitches in each row by knitting two stitches together behind each group of beads (see page 23). Continue as follows:

*K4 \* K2 tog, K5 – repeat from \* to last 4 stitches, K4 (39 stitches).*

*K3 \* sl 3, slip 4 beads, K3 – repeat from \* to the end. K1 row. Repeat the last two rows until there are five rows of four beads spaced across the knitting, with the bead side facing ready for next row.*

*K3 \* K2 tog, K4 – repeat from \* to the end (33 stitches).*

*K3 \* sl 2, slip 3 beads, K3 – repeat from \* to the end. K1 row. Repeat the last two rows until there are three rows of three beads spaced across the knitting, with the bead side facing ready for next row.*

*K3 \* K2 tog, K3 – repeat from \* to end (27 stitches).*

*K3 \* sl 1, slip 2 beads, K3 – repeat from \* to the end. K1 row. Repeat the last two rows twice.*

6 To knit the second side of the bag, continue knitting, repeating steps 3–5 again. To make a bag *without* a flap K2 rows and cast off. To make a bag *with* a flap, continue with the pattern as follows here and in step 7:

*K3 \* sl 1, slip 1 bead, K3 – repeat from \* to the end. K1 row. Repeat the last two rows twice. There will be three rows of single beads spaced across the knitting.*

**7** To knit the little flap for the bag, carry on knitting as follows:

*K3, sl 1, slip 1 bead, K to last 4 stitches, sl 1, slip 1 bead, K3.*

*K3, K2 tog, K to last 5 stitches, K2 tog, K3. Repeat these last two rows until there are 9 stitches left.*

*K3, (K2 tog) twice, K2.*

*K3, sl 1, slip one bead, K3.*

*K3, K2 tog, K2.*

*K row.*

*K1 (K2 tog) twice, K1.*

*K row.*

*K1, K 2 tog, K1, cast (bind) off, leaving a long tail to make the loop fastening.*

## Knitting abbreviations

| K1 | knit 1 stitch |
| K1 row | knit 1 row |
| sl | slip a stitch |
| tog | together |

**8** Make up the bag by folding in half so the two sides match. Using a tapestry needle, oversew the side seams. Sew thread ends into the seams, leaving the thread at the point of the flap.

**9** Sew a small button in the centre front of the purse, about 6mm (¼in) down from the edge. Sew the thread at the point of the flap to make a double loop long enough to fasten around the button. Work blanket stitch (see page 14) over the two threads to strengthen the loop and then sew in the ends to finish.

# You will need

One ball Anchor variegated No.8 coton perlé, colour 1325

One hank of size 11 mid-blue seed beads

Thirty deep blue 4mm (³⁄₁₆in) crystals

Size 0000 (1.25mm) double-pointed knitting needles

Beading needle and tapestry needle

Blue quilting thread

# Try this...

## Fringed purse

This delightful little purse takes on a whole new look for evening if you omit the flap and create a fringe along the bottom, with a strap added for hanging on your wrist or neck.

1 Knit the bag following steps 1–6 on pages 92–93 and then cast (bind) off. Stitch the side seams together with small oversewing stitches.

2 Thread a beading needle with a strong cord thread such as quilting thread, and secure at the right-hand corner of the bag. Pick up 8 seed beads and take the needle through the next centre single bead along the bottom edge. Continue picking up 8 beads and threading through the next centre bead to make loops all along the bottom edge.

3 To create the fringe, at the left-hand corner go back through the last 4 beads threaded, pick up 1 crystal, 8 seed beads, 1 crystal and 1 seed bead. Missing the last seed bead, go back through the 8 seed beads and the crystal bead. Feed the needle through the 4 seed beads up to the bag again ready to add the next fringe. Continue along the loops, adding 4 more seed beads each time until the centre strand has 20 beads and then reduce to shape the fringe on the other side. Sew in the thread ends securely.

4 To make the strap, cut a length of coton perlé long enough for a strap. Thread a crystal bead on to the thread (you should be able to do this without a needle) Transfer 12 seed beads on to the perlé thread (see page 21), thread another crystal bead by hand and then 12 more seed beads. Continue until the strap is the length required, ending with a crystal. Sew the thread ends in at each side of the bag to attach the strap.

# Amulet Purse

Amulet purses come in all sorts of shapes and styles and can be made using a variety of beading techniques, such as bead loom weaving, brick stitch or peyote stitch. These little bags are worked using three-bead netting (see page 17) using two contrasting colours of seed beads that create a subtle two-tone effect. You can reverse the colours of the beads to make two entirely different bags, especially if you make one that closes with loop and tiny blackberry button and the other with a fold-over flap (see page 103 for details).

# You will need

8g size 11 antique seed beads in vanilla ● 8g size 11 antique seed beads in matt cadet blue
● Blue Nymo thread ● White quilting thread ● Two beading needles  (See page 118 for bead details)

1 Refer to page 117 for a diagram of the beading pattern. Cut a 2m (2yd) length of blue Nymo thread and thread a beading needle on each end. Beginning with a blue bead, pick up alternate colours of seed beads until there are 17 beads on the thread. Allow the beads to settle in the middle of the thread and put one needle down. * Pick up 3 white, 1 blue and 1 white bead. Pass the needle through the third last blue bead added. Pick up 1 white, 1 blue and 1 white bead. Miss one blue bead and pass the needle through the next blue bead. Repeat twice more to the second last blue bead. Pick up 1 white and 1 blue bead. Put down the needle.

2 Using the other needle, pick up 3 white beads and pass the needle through the last blue bead added in step 1. Pick up 1 white, 1 blue and 1 white bead and pass the needle through the next blue dropped down bead. Repeat along to the end of the row.

3 Repeat from * (step 1) until there are 8 blue beads down each side of the bead netting, ending with a needle either side.

4 * At one side feed the needle through a white bead and the next drop down blue bead. Work 3 three-bead netting loops across to the other side. Using the same needle, keep working back and forwards, repeating from * reducing the number of loops each time by one until there is only one loop. Secure this thread end with double half hitch knots and sew the thread end into the netting.

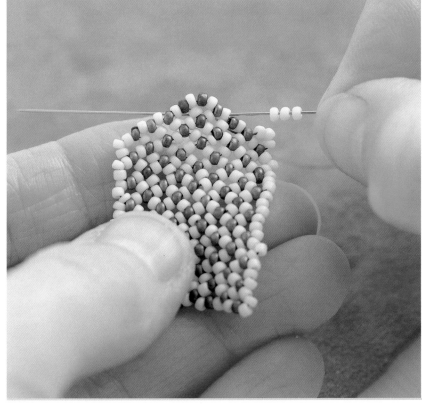

5 Using the other needle, pick up 3 white beads and pass the needle through the third bead along from where the thread comes out. Add six loops in total around the bottom curve of the bag. Feed the needle through the netting to the top of the panel. Work around the curved edge adding 2 white beads between the centre beads in each loop.

6 Pick up a blue bead and feed the needle through the first pair of white beads. Work back around the edge of the bead panel adding a blue bead between each pair of white beads. To allow for the curve of the bag, add an extra blue bead between the pair of white beads at the top of the curve on each side of the panel, opposite the point of the eighth blue bead down each side.

7 The next row begins the netting around the edge of the panel. Pass the needle through the blue bead at the top of the panel. * Pick up 1 blue bead, 1 white and 1 blue bead. Pass the needle through the next blue bead. Repeat from * around the edge of the panel.

8 At the top of the next row, pick up 1 white, 1 blue, 1 white and 1 blue bead and pass the needle through the middle bead in the next loop of netting. This keeps the top of the bag panel level. Continue round to the other side and add another 4 extra beads, as before. Add two further rows of netting to complete the panel.

9 Make a second panel as described in steps 1–8. On both panels, sew in any thread ends securely leaving any long tails at the top edge. Sew the two halves of the bag together by oversewing through every second pair of white beads around the edge of the panel. Pass the needle through the blue beads to the next pair.

10 The strap is worked in a version of chain stitch (see page 20 for instructions). To make the strap, bring a long length of thread out at the top of the side seam. Pass the needle through the 2 white beads, pick up 2 blue beads, 1 white bead and 2 blue beads. Pass the needle through the 2 white beads again then through the next 2 blue beads and the white bead. Pick up 2 blue, 1 white and 2 blue again. Take the needle through the white bead on the previous circle and through the next 2 blue and white beads again. Repeat until the strap is the length required and then sew securely to the top of the side seam.

Work half the strap from each side and join together in the middle.

**11** To finish the bag edge off, bring the needle out below the first pair of white beads. Pick up 6 white beads and feed the needle behind the next pair of white beads. At the bottom pick up only 3 white beads to make a short centre loop and then work back up the other side. Sew in the thread ends securely.

Use quilting thread rather than Nymo thread for the tassel strands so they drape attractively.

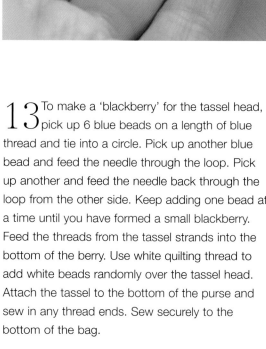

**12** To make the decorative tassel, pick up 14 white beads, miss the bottom bead and feed the needle back through the others. Make a further four tassel strands and tie together.

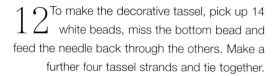

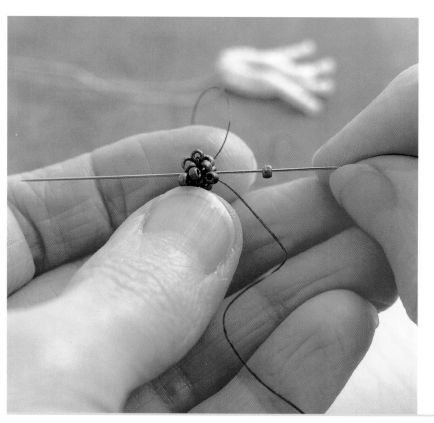

**13** To make a 'blackberry' for the tassel head, pick up 6 blue beads on a length of blue thread and tie into a circle. Pick up another blue bead and feed the needle through the loop. Pick up another and feed the needle back through the loop from the other side. Keep adding one bead at a time until you have formed a small blackberry. Feed the threads from the tassel strands into the bottom of the berry. Use white quilting thread to add white beads randomly over the tassel head. Attach the tassel to the bottom of the purse and sew in any thread ends. Sew securely to the bottom of the bag.

# Fastening the amulet purse...

There are two different ways to make a fastening to close
your amulet purse; both are shown and described here.

## Button and loop fastening

Make a tiny blackberry in the same way as
the tassel head described in step 13 page 102
and then stitch it to the front of the purse.
Using white seed beads, work a small bead
loop on the top edge of the back panel to
complete the fastening.

## Flap fastening

Create a flap for the purse by extending the
netting panel worked in steps 1-3 in the main project.
At step 3 continue adding rows of netting until there
are 11 rather than 8 beads down each side. Work the
shaping of the netting panel, described in step 4, at both
ends to make a long oval shape. Follow the instructions,
working the edging all round the centre panel. At step 9,
line up the front panel on top of the larger back panel
and stitch the sides together. To finish the flap edge,
add loops of 3 contrasting beads around the edge and
secure all thread ends.

# Elegant Evening Bag

If you have a little black dress this elegant beaded bag is just what's needed for that special evening out. Made from a luxurious silver silk dupion, it's decorated with silver and grey beads and sequins. The design is essentially very simple as it is based on a grid of diagonally quilted squares, so if you have an antique bag clasp that you would like to use the design can easily be adapted for an alternative style or shape. The clasp shown is 8cm (3in) wide. If you already have an evening bag, you could make the delightful little purse on page 110 instead.

# You will need

40 x 30cm (16 x 12in) silver silk dupion ● 40 x 30cm (16 x 12in) silk habotai lining fabric ● 40 x 30cm (16 x 12in) cotton backing fabric ● 40 x 30cm (16 x 12in) low-loft wadding (batting) ● 2g each delicas in metallic silver and charcoal grey ● 2g silver-lined hex beads ● Thirteen charcoal grey flat sequins ● 2g size 9 seed beads in light grey and 2g size 11 in dark grey ● Water-soluble fabric marker ● Beading needle ● Metallic silver machine embroidery thread ● Grey sewing thread and quilting thread ● Handbag clasp 8cm (3in) wide (see Suppliers)  (See page 118 for bead details)

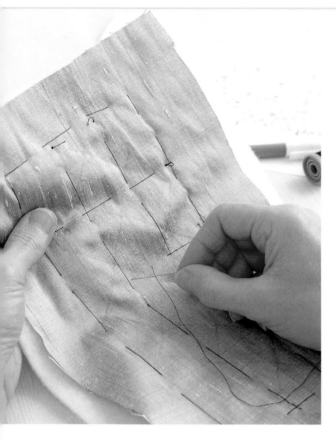

You could stitch the quilting lines using a running stitch and sew the bag by hand using backstitch.

1 Cut two 18 x 28cm (7 x 11in) pieces in silk dupion, wadding (batting) and cotton backing fabric. Copy the template on page 112 and using a light box or holding the fabric and template against a bright window, use a water-soluble marker to trace the diagonal lines and top curve on to the fabric. Make a 'sandwich' of one piece of silk dupion, one piece of wadding (batting) and one piece of backing, and tack (baste) together through all layers.

2 Thread your sewing machine with metallic silver thread on top and grey sewing thread in the bobbin. Stitch around the curve at the top of the bag using a straight stitch, then stitch along all straight lines (see tip, left). Take all thread ends to the reverse side and sew in. Make a second 'sandwich' from silk dupion, wadding and backing and repeat step 2 to make the back of the bag.

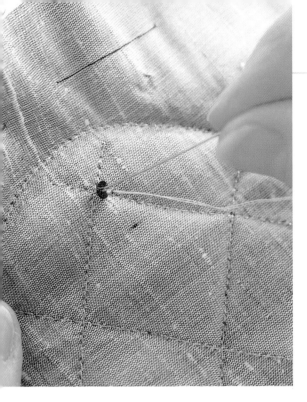

3 Decorate the front panel by first threading a beading needle with a double length of grey sewing thread and bringing it out at one of the points where the quilting threads cross. Pick up a charcoal sequin and a metallic silver delica and take the needle back through the sequin.

4 Bring the needle out at the edge of the sequin at the 12 o'clock position and pick up a metallic silver delica, a silver hex and another metallic silver delica. Take the needle back through at the end so the beads lie flat. Repeat three more times to form a cross. Repeat the motif where each of the quilting threads cross, as shown on the template.

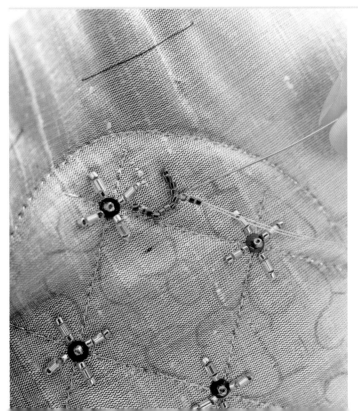

5 Using the template as a guide, draw the curved tendrils inside the first diamond using a water-soluble fabric marker. Using a double length of sewing thread, couch a line of charcoal delicas along each curved line. You can use separate threads to hold the beads and couch down as shown on page 20, or if the line is quite short, use the same thread.

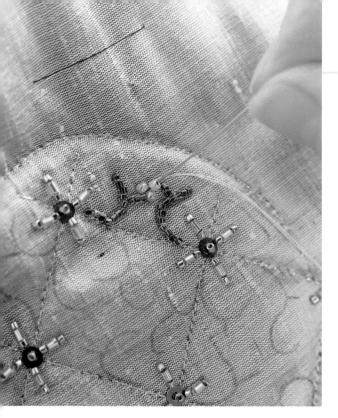

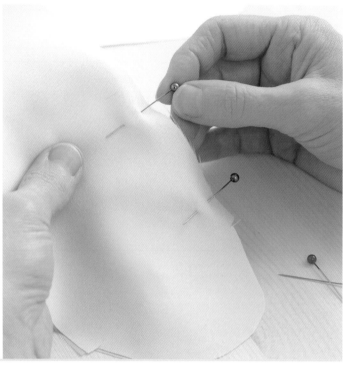

6 Sew 3 individual grey seed beads at the end of the short stems as shown on the template. Continue drawing the design on each diamond and applying beads until the whole area is complete. Spray the fabric to remove the water-soluble marker.

7 To make up the bag, cut two pieces of silk habotai the same shape as the template. Pin the pieces together and stitch along the side and bottom seams.

8 Trim the front and back panels, leaving a 6mm (¼in) seam allowance all round. Pin and tack (baste) the panels, right sides together, and machine stitch the seams using a zip (zipper) foot so you can stitch at the side of the beaded fabric. Trim across the corners.

9 Fit the bag and lining into the bag clasp following the manufacturer's instructions. As the bag frame used here had no sewing holes, two pieces of stiff card were cut to fit along the curves at the top. Craft glue was used to stick the card along the top curve between the lining and bag and the fabric layers were eased into the frame with a teaspoon handle. Ease out the corners along the bottom of the bag and press gently from the back.

If you are using a frame from an old bag, take careful note of how it was assembled when you take it apart.

10 To make a fringe, attach a length of quilting thread securely to one corner of the bag. Pick up 2 dark grey seed beads and 1 charcoal delica, repeat six times and then pick up another 2 dark grey seed beads and 3 silver-lined hex beads. Miss the hex beads and take the needle back through all the previous beads.

11 Take the needle back through where it first emerged and out again 3–6mm (⅛–¼in) along. Repeat the same fringe strands down to the point and back up again to the other side. Sew in the ends securely to finish.

## You will need

6.5cm (2½in) wide gold-coloured purse clasp (see Suppliers)

15cm (6in) square of dark cream silk dupion

15cm (6in) square of ultra-soft heavyweight iron-on interfacing

1g each delicas in matt rose/green and matt dark gold

1g each petite seed beads in metallic gold and rainbow

1g each size 11 rainbow seed beads

Ten 4mm flat sequins in dark grey

Water-soluble pen

Tacking (basting) thread and cream sewing thread

Gold embroidery thread

Beading needle and sewing needle

# Accessorize with this...

## Butterfly purse

Butterflies are an enduring design motif and are ideal for working in bead embroidery. Even in nature the two wings of a butterfly are never identical and so there is no need to worry if the two sides are slightly different.

1 Check the purse clasp fits the top curve on the template on page 117, and adjust if necessary. Using a water-soluble pen, trace the design on to the dark cream silk dupion and then iron a double layer of interfacing on the reverse side. Make a second panel without motif for the reverse side.

2 Couch (see page 20) the beads in place on the butterfly using two separate threads and two needles. Fill the area along the top of the wings with rows of dark gold delicas.

3 Use a rainbow seed bead to attach sequins individually (see photograph). To do this, bring a threaded needle up through the sequin, through the seed bead and back through the sequin. Couch 11 rainbow seed beads around each sequin on the upper wing edges.

4 Outline the body of the butterfly in rose/green delicas and then fill in. Stitch a row of rose/green delicas along the centre line of the wings and down the shorter parallel lines.

5 Fill the area below the curved line with metallic gold petite seed beads and dark gold delicas. Outline the bottom part of the wings with petite rainbow beads and fill in.

6 Sew individual petite rainbow beads every 4mm (³⁄₁₆in) between the top rose/green lines on the wings. Sew rows of 3 petite metallic gold beads in between. Work two lines of split stitch (see page 15) in gold thread along the antennae lines. Spray the fabric to remove the water-soluble marker.

7 Trim the beaded fabric and back panel along the outer template lines. With right sides together, stitch along the inner seam lines using backstitch or machine. Notch the curved seam, snip into the fabric at the end of each seam and turn through. Turn the fabric over along the top curve and tack (baste). Tuck the clasp in position and work tiny prick stitches with a double length of thread to secure the fabric to the clasp.

8 Attach the back panel in the same way. Use the template to cut lining pieces, make up in the same way as the purse and tuck inside. Stitch the lining into the stitches inside the clasp.

# Templates & diagrams

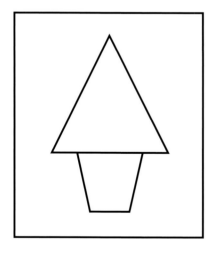

Beaded Gift Bags (page 34)
*templates actual size*

Elegant Evening Bag (page 104)
*template actual size*

Frosted Organza Tote (page 46)
*template actual size*

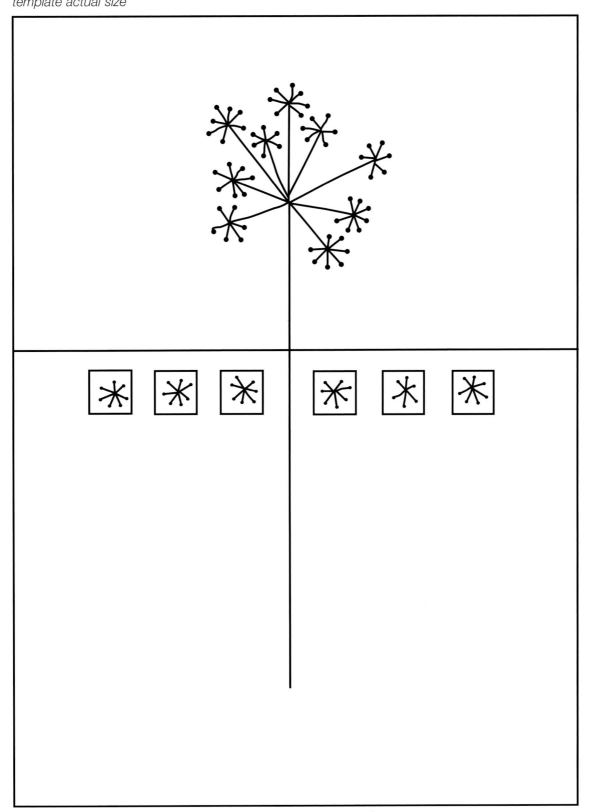

Red Blanket Bag (page 40)
*template actual size*
Match piece A to piece B

A

B

Beaded Gift Bag
Variations (page 39)
*template actual size*

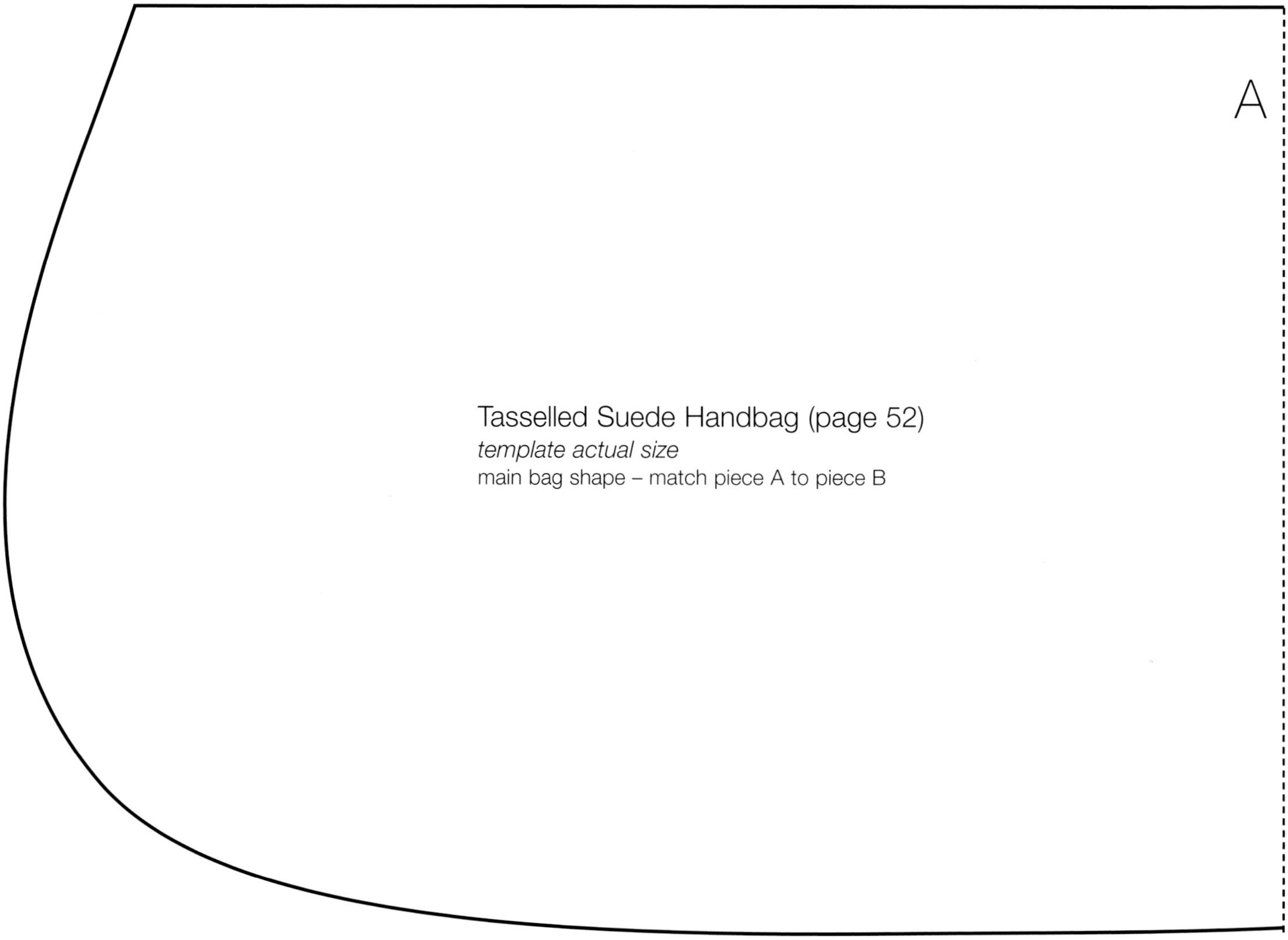

A

Tasselled Suede Handbag (page 52)
*template actual size*
main bag shape – match piece A to piece B

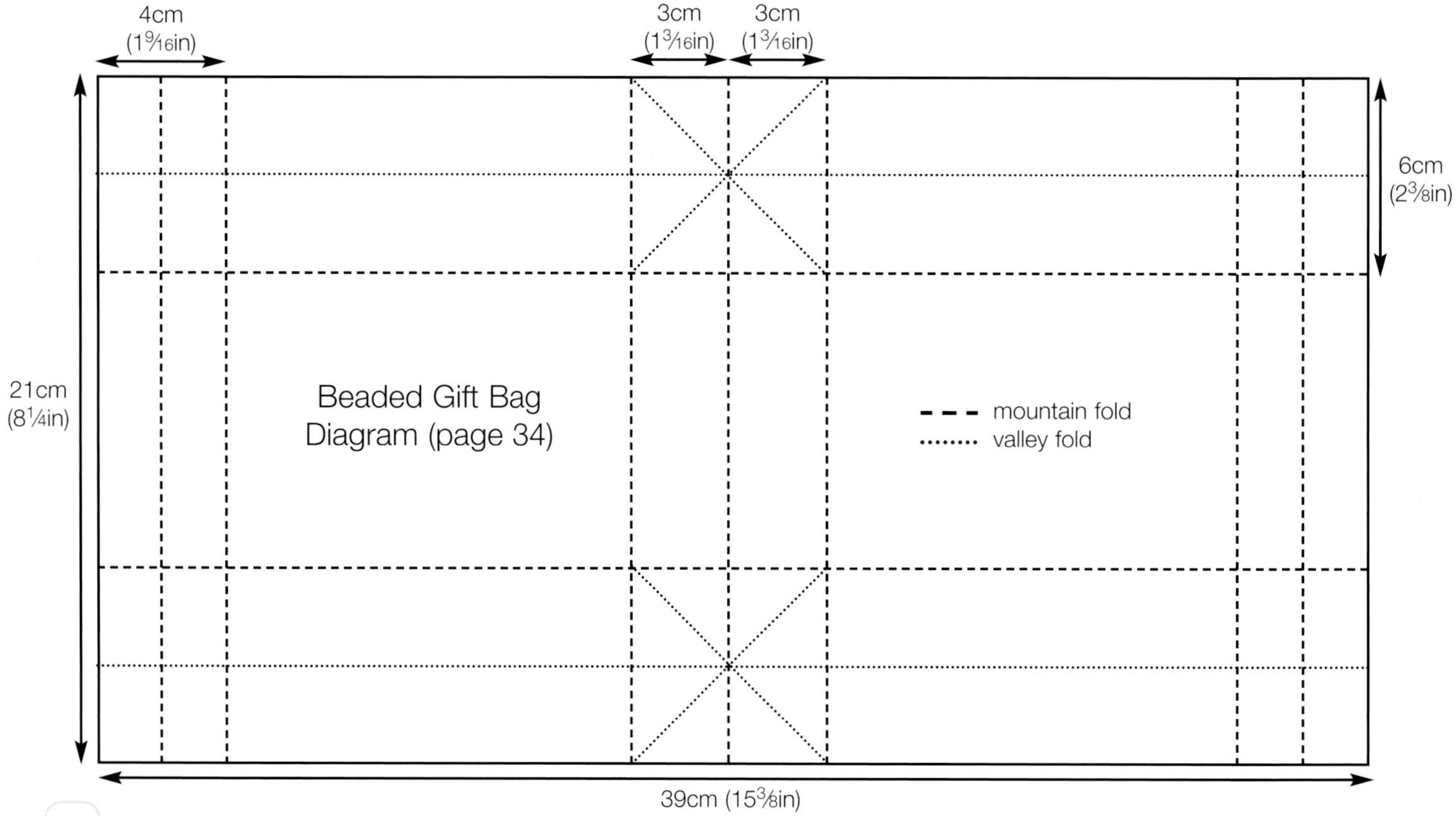

4cm
(1⁹⁄₁₆in)

3cm
(1³⁄₁₆in)

3cm
(1³⁄₁₆in)

6cm
(2³⁄₈in)

21cm
(8¹⁄₄in)

Beaded Gift Bag
Diagram (page 34)

– – – mountain fold
......... valley fold

39cm (15³⁄₈in)

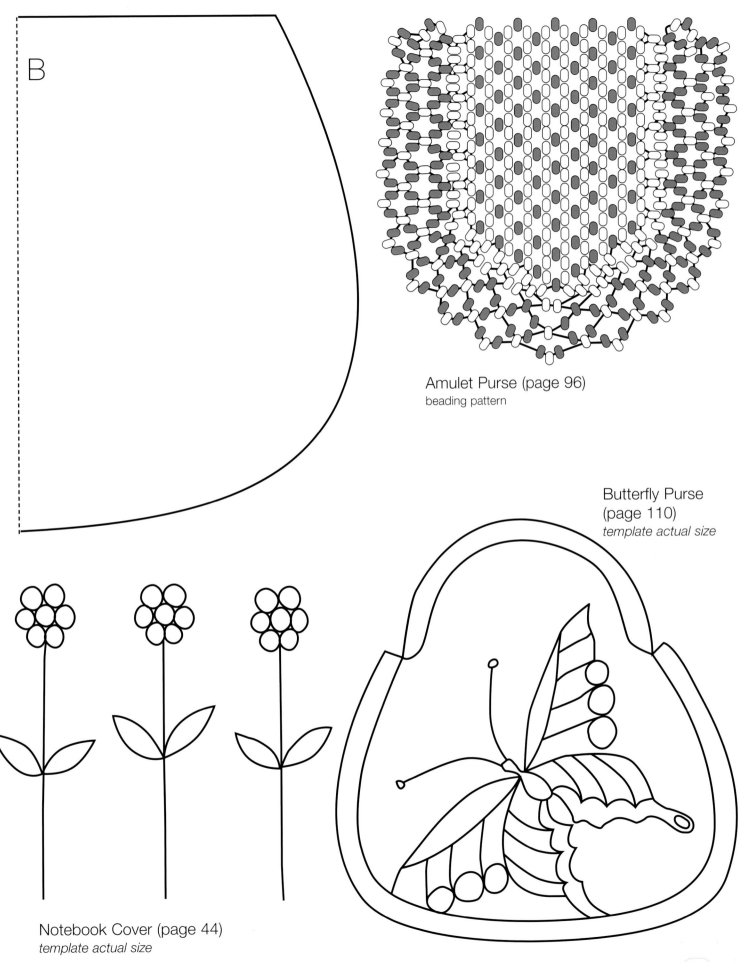

B

Amulet Purse (page 96)
beading pattern

Butterfly Purse
(page 110)
*template actual size*

Notebook Cover (page 44)
*template actual size*

# Bead project details

This list contains details of the various beads and accessories used in the projects, giving their specific colours and codes. The list is correct at the date of publication, but the availability of beads can change. The list of suppliers on the facing page will help in sourcing the beads and accessories for your project.

**Flower Beach Bag (page 28)**
*Constellation Beads*
Satin-finish seed beads and bugles – navy, cerise and turquoise. Flower beads – peacock.

**Cotton Tote (page 32)**
*Creative Beadcraft Ltd*
Ceramic beads – pink, red, silver, lilac and cerise (CC19).

**Beaded Gift Bags (page 34)**
*The London Bead Company*
Seed beads – pink-lined (255) and lime crystal (239).

**Red Blanket Bag (page 40)**
*21st Century Beads*
Melon and 6mm (¼in) round wood beads – black.

**Frosted Organza Tote (page 46)**
*Mill Hill Beads*
Petite seed beads – ivory (40123).
Bugle beads – ivory (70123).

**Handbag Mirror (page 51)**
*Mill Hill Beads*
Petite seed beads – matt chocolate (42038) and ivory (40123).

**Tasselled Suede Handbag (page 52)**
*Mill Hill Beads*
Seed beads – black (02014).
Bugle beads – black (72014, 82014 and 92014).

**Elegant Tassel (page 59)**
*Mill Hill Beads*
Seed beads – ivory (40123).
Bugle beads – ivory (70123, 80123 and 90123).

**Ribbon Shoe Bag (page 60)**
*Perivale-Gütermann Ltd*
Seed beads – aubergine (5435).
Pyramid crystals – pale pink (5185).

**Luxury Lattice Purse (page 68)**
*Perivale-Gütermann Ltd*
Seed beads – aqua (7500), mauve (5655) and rainbow (5470).
Faceted 4mm – aqua (7300) and lilac (5505).

**Glasses Case (page 73)**
*Perivale-Gütermann Ltd*
Seed beads – aqua (7500), deep blue (6530) and blue (7230).
Metallic flower beads (5723).

**Crochet Shopper (page 74)**
*21st Century Beads*
Round wood beads 6mm – orange.

**Make-up Bag (page 80)**
*Creative Beadcraft Ltd*
Ceramic beads – pink, red, silver, lilac and cerise (CC19).

**Dreamy Bridal Bag (page 82)**
*Perivale-Gütermann Ltd*
Seed beads – clear (1030) and white (1016).
Crystal beads 4mm – clear (1016) and white matt (1016).
Pyramid beads 6mm – clear (1016).
Teardrop beads – 3mm clear (1016) and 5mm clear (1016).
Pearls 4mm – white (1030).

**Bridal Tiara (page 88)**
*Beads as for bridal bag, above.*

**Knitted Pouch (page 90)**
*Viking Loom*
Seed bead strings size 11 – pink-lined.

**Fringed Purse (page 95)**
*Viking Loom*
Seed bead strings size 11 – mid blue.
*Perivale-Gütermann Ltd*
Crystals 4mm – deep blue (5960).

**Amulet Purse (page 96)**
*Mill Hill Beads*
Antique seed beads – vanilla (03016) and matt cadet blue (03046).

**Elegant Evening Bag (page 104)**
*The London Bead Company*
Flat sequins 4mm – charcoal grey.
Silver-lined hex beads (034).
Delicas – palladium-plated (038) and charcoal-lined (925).
Seed beads – silver-lined ice blue (42) and black-tinted lustre (262).

**Butterfly Purse (page 110)**
*Mill Hill Beads*
Seed beads – Victorian copper (42030) and rainbow (40374).
Petite seed beads – rainbow (00374).
*The London Bead Company*
Flat sequins 4mm – charcoal grey.
*Beadbox*
Delicas – rose/green metallic (D380) and matt dark gold (D334).

# Suppliers

## UK suppliers

**The Bead Merchant**
PO Box 5025, Coggleshall, Essex
CO6 1HW
tel: 01376 563 567
fax: 01376 563 568
www.beadmerchant.co.uk

**21st Century Beads**
Craft Workshops, South Pier Road,
Ellesmere Port, Cheshire CH65 4FW
tel: 0151 356 4444
fax: 0151 355 3377
email: sales@beadmaster.com
www.beadmaster.com

**Constellation Beads**
PO Box 88, Richmond,
North Yorkshire DL10 4FT
tel: 01748 826552
fax: 01748 826552
email: info@constellationbeads.co.uk
www.constellationbeads.co.uk

**Coats Crafts UK**
PO Box 22, Lingfield, McMullen Road,
Darlington, County Durham DL1 1YQ
tel: 01325 365457
*For variegated coton perlé, fine
knitting needles and eyelets*

**Creative Beadworks Ltd**
Denmark Works, Sheepcote Dell
Road, Beaumond End, nr Amersham,
Buckinghamshire HP7 0RX
tel: 01494 778818
email: beads@creativebeadcraft.co.uk
www.creativebeadcraft.co.uk

**Framecraft Miniatures Ltd**
(for Mill Hill beads)
Lichfield Road, Brownhills, Walsall,
West Midlands WS8 6LH
tel: 01543 360 842
fax: 01543 453 154
email: sales@framecraft.com
www.framecraft.com

**Gütermann Beads**
For nearest stockist:
Perivale-Gütermann Ltd, Bullsbrook
Road, Hayes, Middlesex UB4 0JR
tel: 0208 589 1600
fax: 0208 589 1644
UK email: perivale@guetermann.com
Europe email: mail@guetermann.com

**John Lewis**
Nationwide chain of department stores
tel: 0845 604 9049 for stores and
website ordering details
*For wools, yarns, fabrics, ribbons and
a wide range of craft products*

**The London Bead Company**
339 Kentish Town Road, Kentish
Town, London NW5 2TJ
tel: 0207 267 9403
fax: 0207 284 2062
email: londonbead@dial.pipex.com
www.londonbeadco.co.uk
*Beads and also handbag clasps*

**Neumann Leathers**
New Victoria Mill, Wellington St Bury,
Manchester BL8 2AL
tel: 0161 763 1149
fax: 0161 763 1152
email: sales@neumannleathers.co.uk
www.neumannleathers.com

**The Scientific Wire Company**
18 Raven Road, London E18 1HW
tel: 0208 505 0002
fax: 0208 559 1114
email: dan@wires.co.uk
www.wires.co.uk

**The Viking Loom**
22 High Petergate, York Y01 7EH
tel/fax: +44 (0)1904 765599
email: vikingloom@vikingloom.co.uk
www.vikingloom.co.uk
*For handbag clasps and seed bead
strings*

## US suppliers

**Bag Lady Press**
PO Box 2409, Evergreen
CO 80437-2409
tel: (303) 670 2177
fax: (303) 670 2179
email: baglady@baglady.com
www.baglady.com
*For bag clasps and fine knitting needles*

**Beadbox**
1290 N. Scottsdale Road, Tempe
Arizona 85281-1703
tel: 1-800-232-3269
fax: 1-800-242-3237
www.beadbox.com

**Gütermann of America Inc**
8227 Arrowbridge Blvd, PO Box 7387
Charlotte NC 28241-7387
tel: (704) 525 7068
fax: (704) 525 7071
email: info@gutermann-us.com

**Mill Hill Beads**
For nearest stockist:
Gay Bowles Sales Inc, PO Box 1060,
Janesville, WI, 53547-1060
tel: (608) 754-9466
fax: (608) 754-0665
www.millhill.com

# Acknowledgments

I would like to thank the following companies for so generously supplying beads and accessories for this book: Constellation Beads, Framecraft Miniatures (UK) Ltd, Gay Bowles Sales Inc., Perivale-Gütermann, The London Bead Company, 21st Century beads and The Viking Loom.

Thanks to the editorial team who gave me lots of support and made a superb job of putting the book together – Cheryl, Jennifer and Lin and, finally, thanks to Simon Whitmore for the wonderful photography, taken at Ashwell Barn in Devon and to designer, Prudence Rogers, who have made this such a beautiful book.

# About the author

Dorothy Wood is a talented and prolific craft maker and author. Since completing a course in Advanced Embroidery and Textiles at Goldsmith's College, London, she has written seventeen craft books, and contributed to another twenty, on all kinds of subjects. This is Dorothy's third book published by David & Charles, her first being the best-selling *Simple Glass Seed Beading*. Dorothy also contributes to several well-known craft magazines, including *Crafts Beautiful*. She lives in the small village of Osgathorpe, Leicestershire, UK.

# Index